MW01061708

SPRING RAIN

OTHER BOOKS BY
MARC HAMER

How to Catch a Mole:
Wisdom from a Life Lived in Nature

Seed to Dust:
Life, Nature, and a Country Garden

Spring Rain

A Life Lived in Gardens

Marc Hamer

GREYSTONE BOOKS
VANCOUVER/BERKELEY/LONDON

Greystone Books Ltd.
greystonebooks.com

Cataloguing data available from Library and Archives Canada
ISBN 978-1-77840-027-8 (cloth)
ISBN 978-1-77840-028-5 (epub)

Jacket and text design by Jessica Sullivan
Jacket illustration by Karine Daisay
Proofreading by Jennifer Stewart

This book is substantially a work of non-fiction based on the life, experiences and
recollections of the author. In some limited cases, names of people and places and
the sequences of events have been changed solely to protect the privacy of others.

Printed and bound in Canada on FSC® certified paper at Friesens. The FSC®
label means that materials used for the product have been responsibly sourced.

Greystone Books thanks the Canada Council for the Arts, the British Columbia
Arts Council, the Province of British Columbia through the Book Publishing Tax
Credit, and the Government of Canada for supporting our publishing activities.

Canadä

Greystone Books gratefully acknowledges the xʷməθkʷəy̓əm (Musqueam),
Sḵwx̱wú7mesh (Squamish), and səlilwətaɬ (Tsleil-Waututh) peoples on
whose land our Vancouver head office is located.

Contents

'Do what thou wilt,'
my grandmother told me,
'but harm none.'

All the moments arrive,
the past and present intertwine.
In this brief spell, the brief rose blooms and dies,
a brief life passes by, the brief trees grow and
    stand, then fall.

There is of course no beginning. There is no end. A story starts when you want to start telling it and stops when you want to finish. That's the way it is with everything. This is a story about the rain, a boy, an angry dog and a gardener and how some of them find peace and freedom. I wrote it for the oddballs, the ones like me; it is a true story and I want it to start here . . .

RAIN

An adventure at sea, treasure island, a little wooden hut

✻ ❀ ✻ ❀

A small boy in grey school shorts stands on tiptoe. He is around seven years old. Jelly-bean toes in plastic sandals kick against the battered skirting board as he looks through the window. He is slim, tall for his age, with a little soft belly under his white school shirt, which is untucked, the sleeves rolled up, the shorts cinched to his waist with a blue-and-red elastic belt fastened with a metal hook designed to look like a snake. He loves his snake belt and wears it whenever he can, likes to feel the texture of the scales stamped into its shiny metal skin, to scratch his finger-nails along its ridges and hollows and look into the two rough circles of its eyes; he feels he has some company when it's there. His pale eyes are set in a serious face under pure-white hair, his body is loose and perfect, his face is noticeably symmetrical and harmonious, but perhaps a lit-tle too intense. He leans his chin on tanned arms, folded on the heavy wooden window-ledge that's been thickly painted, creamy white over the chips and ripples of older layers. Through the window of this unloved rented house he watches rain pound on the shiny road so hard that each marble-sized drop makes a ring of waves and bounces up, then lands again to make another smaller, tender splash in its own rippling target. The boy and his family have just moved house again, and once more it's mess and loss and new things and places to learn about. It has always been like this.

The rain slows, then stops. The garden at the back of the house is completely flooded after weeks of downpour, brown muddy water coming up to the bottom of the kitchen step. Twigs and leaves and little bits of wood and soil lie on its still and greasy surface, and the meniscus that laps each sliver of detritus catches a silvery light from the sky. A flock of sparrows sing in the damson tree and a 'plink, plink, plink' of drops fall from its leaves into the water below. At the far end of the garden, and raised above the water on a base of bricks, there's an old wooden shed, its single square eye looking sadly at the house. As it is isolated on its island, nobody has been able to visit it since they moved in.

Among the piles of packing cases filled with pots and pans and bags of bedding squatting in the hall is a heavy old plastic tub, opal white and scratched along the bottom, where it has been dragged in and out of a cupboard under one set of stairs or another for years. It was used for the washing of babies—three of them, one after the other, two years apart. He remembers his mother's long arms leaning down over him as she let him 'help' her wash the youngest one. She seems, in his mind, to be mostly arms growing from a big ball of curly brown hair, lots of busy arms.

He mooches about as an idea grows; he's bored and wants adventure. The garden lake, the baby's bath, the water lapping at the step. Aristotle said that nature hates a vacuum, so the flood and bath are sucked into the emptiness of his day. In his mind—its job reversed—the tub is outside, floating, holding water out, instead of inside holding water in. Marvelling that this one thing can do two completely opposite jobs, he drags the bath through the house, knocking it against the battered doorways, to the kitchen step, slides it down the granite block and it bobs, almost eagerly, among the flotilla of twigs and half-rotted leaves and rainbow swirls of oil and cracked black sky reflected. Wobbling himself into this opalescent coracle, he sits with knees drawn up and pushes himself along with the peeling, red-painted head of a stiff-bristled yard brush that had been floating by. It is hard work, but he knows where he wants to go and not even the growing wind will turn him back.

He sails like a boy in the moon across the reflected sky towards the safety of the ship that waits abandoned, beached, drawing him magnetically close. His tiny tender scrapes the path below the shallow muddy lake and then along the softer bed of submerged grass that waves against the hull, until he gets to deeper water where the seabed falls away and his pearly shell of a boat wobbles and feels like it will tilt, then fill and be overwhelmed and sink down to the slimy deep. He has to push down hard to stay upright as he draws closer to safety.

You emerge from the best of adventures with a completely new 'self' and this was the beginning of one of the very best. He didn't care if he died, and so on. Every real adventure begins that way, I think.

With its stone slab step, the tiny wooden hut has a ready-made jetty to dock at. The boat bumps into the haven and the boy crawls out on hands and knees, stands and pulls at the stiff warped door while the bath drifts carelessly away in the breeze and he blends into the shadows of this dark, damp wonder, without a thought of how he'll get back home. Here's an ark that can save him, a cathedral of peace, the private space he craves so very much, like the whale sent to Jonah to rescue him from the maelstrom of misery and storm.

The boards of the wooden floor are stained and dark with years of passing boots and spilled viscous liquids, scattered with the rolling leaden spheres of desiccated woodlice. The milky window is draped with the torn grey nets of ancient spider webs that tattered, swaying in a breeze above a dark-brown bench with rings where old tins stood. He smells the sweet metallic richness of rust, the dark mystery of soil and engine oil, paraffin, paint, rotten wood, insinuating mushrooms and creosote. It is a place where things have been done in peace, things made or mended with workmanlike intent, alone, and private journeys taken. Sniffing, he can focus on the mushroom smell or tar or rotting iron and play one scent against the other, or blend them like an organ in his head.

Over thirty minutes or a lifetime while he's there, the sun slips down to join the earth, the inky sky begins to part and show the evening's first and brightest stars as the inside of this whale grows dark and dives into the depths of night. His mother calls his name, sounding irritated, irritating the air, grating his nerves, and he wants to sink down safe inside the wooden ribs, but knows he can't refuse her siren pull. He goes to the step, tests the depth of water with a stick and, instead of trying somehow to get the ferry back to the mainland, knowing he should hurry, he takes off his sandals and wades through the brown sea, which at the deepest part laps at his knees almost to the hem of his short trousers. Feeling unknowable things beneath his toes that squish and horrify him, he tries to run against the resistance of the water.

'Get changed, put your shorts in the wash and put your bloody sandals by the oven before your father comes down, then come down for tea,' she says. Shaking her head at her idiot son, who is too far gone into his own world to be worth rescuing. She wonders if he can be saved, he's always been . . . the word she finally accepts, after cycling through a number of less-than-generous terms, is 'different'.

He doesn't answer. If he were to say 'okay' or 'yes, Mum', it could possibly be taken in the wrong way and he could be accused of 'having an attitude' or 'answering back', so he makes himself appear busy and runs to do as he is told. Invisibility really is the key to a comfortable life; all good prey animals know how to hide.

HIS MOTHER OFTEN seems far away, her mind in a distant world she pines for somewhere way over there, over the horizon, over the rainbow. As if there are things in the way that she is trying to see beyond, the things that come after the cooking and shopping and the day-to-day, and day after day of nothing but this.

His father is an angry dog who, when he is not sleeping, is barking, growling or sulking, reacting to each tiny thing.

He thinks control is manly. The boy knows not to prod him or disturb him when he dozes, to creep around him as quietly as possible. The Angry Dog looks dimly at his little world and ponders his misery.

'What's going on in your head, boy?' he barks.

'Nothing, just eating my dinner,' he replies and tries to look happy.

Angry Dog shakes his head, lets out a low growl and settles to his meal, and the boy smiles inside at the hound-like image of him, chomping at his bowl.

People think of children as fragile vessels like bottles, or as flappingly empty bags that need filling with whatever we decide we want them to carry. We can use them as receptacles and brainwash them into sharing our beliefs, but they don't really need us adults nearly as much as we would like to think. Children are designed to work out how the world works in order to survive. They do this in their own way and rarely turn out the way we imagine they will before they are born.

Gerberas, umbrella, zinc, guilt, bow tie

I am sitting on a bench and waiting for Peggy; we have been away for a few days and she has gone to the library to do some research for her new book. I do all my research in cafés, on trains and park benches. I am looking forward to seeing my lover again, but mixed with that excitement is another, more complicated emotion, a happy/sad feeling, as if I were watching my first child going through the school gates on his initial day and leaving me. The mixed emotions that come with a change of identity. I used to be a gardener, but I don't do that any more because I am too old. They called me 'The Gardener'—'The Gardener is here,' they might say to each other when I arrived. Perhaps I should try to figure out what I am now and what my life is for; that would be the normal thing to do, I suppose, but as the idea comes, it goes. This is the way it is with me: thoughts arise and screech, then pass like gulls and I'm often pleased to see them go.

On my lap is a bunch of bright-orange gerberas that I bought from the florist across the road. A special door opens when I have flowers, which takes me, each time I look at them, into a place where I and they are not owner and owned, but a mirror to each other. This is because flowers change at a pace I can understand, they brown and fall and whisper at the thinnest edge of my awareness that I am good and beautiful, even though I fade and wilt. I look at them and I see myself a flower.

I like to have flowers, that is how it is, on my table while I eat, by my chair where I sit and read or in my hand while I wait for my love to arrive. Peggy often brings me flowers. I would wear one in my buttonhole, but I know that I look odd enough already, so I prefer to just hold them. When I do, ladies look at me and smile—I like that.

Outside the shop across the road, where I bought them, there is a three-tiered stand made of wooden slats on a metal frame; once they were painted forest green, but now they're old and flaked and show layers of battleship grey, white and seaside blue. The galvanised buckets on the stand are the colour of the dented zinc sky. Hanging around in containers, drooping and flopping, are the stems of twisted willow, pale winter lilies, white and pink roses and heavy rusty chrysanthemums. The brightest things around, aglow on their tottering stalks, stand out from the concrete walls and street and from people passing in front who hide, then reveal, then hide them again.

The thin municipal trees behind my bench are bare. I have a scarf and gloves, and my jacket and trousers are warm and my socks are thick. I am always early, so a while ago I wandered over to buy the flowers and I went into the old-fashioned 'gentlemen's outfitters' next door, the kind of shop I like to buy my clothes from. Among the button braces and shirts, tweed jackets, moleskin waistcoats, knitted tank tops and corduroy trousers, smelling of natural fabrics that used to be living things—wool and cotton and dust—I found a little shelf with a stack of rectangular boxes the size of a mobile phone and three times as thick. Black cardboard with a clear plastic top, with swirly gold 1970s writing that said, '*Monsieur Paul*'. On the end of the boxes the prices were written on a white label in hard grey pencil in the kind of flowing handwriting you don't see any more, done by people who had learned to write at school with a pen they dipped in ink, the writing of really old people: £14.99. The boxes had been there for years, their cardboard corners crushed, fibres of white showing through the cracks. Through the transparent lids the colours and patterns of the bow ties inside showed. Dark red, deep blue, green tartan, paisley, stripes and spots. Old, thick silk in muted colours.

I bought a narrow blue one with white spots and square ends, took off my long striped tie and rolled it up in my top jacket pocket, leaving a bit sticking out. After a few attempts at the speckled mirror, I managed to get the bow tie almost right, if a little lopsided. In the world of bow ties, it is important that it should be ever so slightly imperfect; this is to show that: a) you tied it yourself; and b) that you are slightly 'devil may care' and not at all prissy. Perfection is the sign of an amateur, perhaps someone who works with great skill but without connection to his animal nature, to passion and lust. Perfection is not for living things, certainly not for human beings; if you are not capable of loving flaws and faults, then you are not capable of love. I have lived most of my life in poverty, but I can tie a bow tie and to some this will be a mystery, but anybody who knows me would say, 'Of course he can tie a bow tie.' Such imperfections—wrinkles in the world—are where all of life's best stories are.

WHEN I WAS twenty-four I walked away from my job on the railway. I've always considered myself a vagrant just passing through. I was a guard on coal trains, riding alone in a brake van as we rattled through the night from one coal yard to another, past curtained lamplit windows of houses by the line-side; I was black with coal dust, and I always had a grubby paperback in my pocket and read Plath and Orwell, Steinbeck and Lawrence, Kerouac and Richard Bach and many more who became my friends, by a small oil lamp swinging on a chain while being jolted this way and that and writing in a filthy notebook. I'd been there seven years and had had enough. I was hungry for an education—I had left school at fifteen and was indiscriminately reading everything I could get my hands on; I needed to learn what to read. I wanted to be a poet and I needed a new adventure, I was bored and didn't care if I lived or died, and so on. So I handed in my lamp and watch and went to a local college, working part-time in a hospital and cooking in a chicken shop at night. My art teacher there told me to apply to art school. I didn't know anybody who had stayed on at school beyond fifteen, let alone become a student, but I wanted to learn everything I could and, with those bits of paper and a portfolio of drawings and photographs, I was able to go and study art and . . . well, it's a bit like poetry, isn't it?

I worked in the chicken shop with a Frenchman, an anarchist who kept a loaded gun at the bottom of his wardrobe. Jean-Marc always wore a dark suit and tie, even when he was cooking. I'd crashed and ruined my motorcycle, but with money saved from my job on the railway I bought a Land Rover and we cruised around in that. We cooked burgers and chickens together, read Marx and Kropotkin and drank a lot, and eventually shared an unheated cold-water flat. It was bitter cold in the winter and we put on layers of clothes and sat around a little electric fan heater to drink the champagne and wine he brought back from his trips to Paris. We had decided that buying champagne was a better use of our chicken-shop money than paying electricity bills, so we stayed cold and got drunk and wore overcoats.

During the day I went to art school and wrote poetry and painted great massive abstract colour fields like Mark Rothko, and big heavy pictures made of sacking and plaster and lead like Antoni Tàpies, because they made me feel peaceful and I liked them. It was an uncomplicated life that made sense—an anarchic student life of painting, drinking, sit-ins, love-ins and protests. I bought my clothes second-hand and also started to wear a suit because: a) they were cheap and I was poor, and they often seemed nearly new and I didn't want to be scruffy any more; b) I was an art student; c) I liked to look minimal, like an anarchist, even if I was vague on many principles beyond the rejection of authority, which I was already a master of; and d) as two young men serving burgers wearing suits, we thought we looked pretty cool. Of course a suit needs a tie, and an artist/poet in particular should have a bow tie, so I bought one from the wire basket in a charity shop and learned to tie it from the instructions on the back of the box it was still in; it was yellow silk with a geometric pattern and had never been worn. So that's how and why I learned to tie a bow tie.

I'M SITTING ON a bench near the railway station, an old anarchist in a suit and bow tie (I've always had ideas above my station), with a big bunch of flowers because the day felt grubby and dull and I thought that life deserved celebrating. There's nothing else to do with life but celebrate it, believe me; I am old, and there's truly nothing other to do with life than celebrate the fact that it exists.

I came to town to meet Peggy because I thought she might like it if I met her, and if I looked nice when I did so. She will smile when she sees me and remember that I love her. You have to smile at an old man in a bow tie.

I like to follow the path that nature gives me. Much of what happens in life is not in my power; most events are the outcome of stuff that happened thousands of years ago and will have outcomes of their own in years to come.

I adapt and enjoy and refuse to fight the things that can't be fought, I let go of the questions that cannot be answered and instead I push at doors that fall open to my touch and ignore the ones that resist too much. I have worked hard, tried hard, learned that life has flow and that resisting it brings problems. I've known people who fight too hard for what they want—fighting and wanting become a way of life and they never stop and never get happy. I ride streams that are going my way, share moments with people who are friendly, stroke relaxed dogs and approachable cats, cut the grass when the sun shines, shelter when it rains, and so on. Instead of standing in the ocean and feeling its swell pushing at me, trying to resist its push and then staggering and falling, I like to lift my feet just a little and be lifted. Bobbing effortlessly along like a leaf in a rill, turning this way and that to look at the world as it passes—enjoying the ride. That doesn't mean simply accepting the ways of people. Injustice, cruelty and greed must be addressed, but I try to do it with love, with understanding and compassion. Not to confront, but to gently open a better, kinder desire-path for the stream to flow into because it's easier. Some people, of course, are beyond the ability to change and so must be resisted. It's not all plain sailing.

I wasn't always a follower of the path. I wanted to be a writer and I tried so hard, entering, applying, but the doors remained so tightly closed that my knuckles bled from knocking. Then I gave up fighting and fell in love again with life, wrote the poetry of my days and the things that woke me in the early hours, demanding to be held in the mind for a moment and be seen. Now I don't care about 'being' anything, I like writing for fun. Desire got in the way and slowed me down. I do what the moment tells me to do, instinctively. Of course I make plans of a vague, uncertain kind but I'm not overly attached to them.

A quick rain from a blue sky, long and thin and lit from above by scudding clouds. The leaves rattle as they are tapped, wind-blown like crinkling paper. Little spots on the brown wax-shine of my shoes catch the light. The rain creates a nice quiet space, calms everything down. It is a gift. When I press the button on the side of my umbrella, it clicks and opens slowly like a flower with a hesitation that pleases me, as if it would rather stay curled up, nested and dry. I've forced it out to protect me and I smile at my pang of guilt. We are both things that get set into action by outside influences, both parts of a long chain of cause and effect.

Under my friendly vaulted roof the drips swell on the shiny metal tips until they are fat and full; they catch the sunlight; fall and land on the still-dry paving stones as dark and shiny circles, scattered chocolate coins, fish scales, cherry blossom, melted jewels at my feet. Sitting and waiting for Peggy and listening to the growing spatter of rain on the massed waxy leaves of evergreens behind, and its plop-plop-plop amplified by the drum-skin of my nylon umbrella, I feel sanctified, made holy, in love, and that feels enough. What a joy it is, now that I don't have to labour, to look out at the rain.

From my bench I can see that the world has created:

1. Two magpies
2. A black-and-white cat sheltering under a parked car
3. Three old seagulls and one young one
4. What sounds like at least forty sparrows in the holly tree behind me; they are singing in the rain
5. Very many jackdaws—I love the blue of their eyes
6. Dandelions between the paving stones. Some moss.

It has been quiet for a while but a train has just arrived. A crowd begins to build, some people stand out from the moving flow like cherries in a slice of cake; a woman limps by wearing a mustard-coloured suede boot on her left foot and a swooshed trainer on her right—she has an injured foot that's bandaged up; she carries a paper coffee cup and hobbles quickly, leaning. A man in striped trousers and a ponytail wears a dark jacket with three buttons; white soles; yellow socks; pink satin tie shining in the sun. A hipster girl with short red hair and red Doc Martens, riding a Dutchie. A black woman with massive Afro hair and bright lipstick—gorgeous in a peony-print scarf. A woman in a yellow coat and tightly bobbed black hair trundles a fuchsia wheelie-case. A pretty woman in square dark-rimmed glasses and narrow trousers, smiling in the rain and riding a blue bike. A handsome man in navy corduroy trousers, a green knitted waistcoat underneath his jacket and wearing glamorous spectacles, leads an elegant dog, balletic in a berry coat and an egg-yellow collar. They are all rushing a little because of the rain, but it's not too heavy. They stand out from the crowd, these generous souls, reflected in the wet stone pavement, these flowers in the garden who freely share their colour and life with everyone around; they do it because they enjoy it, they cannot prevent themselves from flowering, these hardy, happy rebels who refuse to live in fear of what the downcast say. I cannot help smiling. They blossom and it's all worthwhile—everything is worthwhile.

If you watch people long enough, you will fall in love with them. I like to watch people but they don't like to be watched, they think you see their imperfections and, having seen them, judge them as harshly as they judge themselves. On their faces there is often pain, loss, anger, fear, but there's joy and love too, and reaching out. Three girls are smiling at each other, two men holding hands, groups hugging, lovers and friends. They are beautiful, heroic in infinite ways; they all struggle up fiery mountains, each of them battles with demons to realise the same simple things: love, unity, peace. They know we are better together but don't know how, nobody knows how.

The people seem to go by almost silently with just a little splashing but no talking or other sounds. It is one of those weirdly quiet days when although there are lots of people around, the air feels dense and solid and silent, as if the rain were insulating us. Portentous, as if something is about to happen. If I keep looking, stay alert, I think the world will present me with a new adventure.

RAIN

Tools, seeds,
a cleaning song, books
and a train to nowhere

A FLOODED GARDEN

The tide has gone out and left the path to the shed covered in a thick layer of mud, which will wash away when the next rain comes. The boy opens the cupboard under the stairs where the shoes and coats and cleaning things are jumbled together, dumped like a pile of coal in an unlit bunker; he fills his arms with a sweeping brush, a dustpan and some rags and carries them gingerly down the slippery path to the shed.

When he punted his coracle through the gap between downpours he could not have imagined the treasure he would find. In the shed there is a workbench against the window with a vice on the end, an ancient dark-brown wooden stool with a circular top and turned legs patinated with a monumental sheen of dusty green mould. The bench has a drawer in the middle with a keyhole and a round wooden knob that wobbles loosely as he tugs it. Inside, some rusty old tools; secateurs that will not open; pliers in the same condition; a small tack hammer; a tin box with old packets of seeds in it: radish, lettuce, kale; some keys—he tries them all, but none of them fits the drawer. He puts them all back where they came from and begins to clean up.

As he brushes the floor and dusts the bench and shelves, he remembers part of a song that he heard on the radio, the only shed song he can think of. He knows the tune but only a few bits of the first line, he has to make the rest of it up; his memory will never be good, but he likes words and enjoys inventing songs and rhymes. He sings as he polishes the window with the rags and brushes away the cobwebs, in a sweet little voice:

'I want to keep,
my little wooden hut from you-ooo
The rain,
is coming and I don't need you-ooo
I'm si-tting,
on my little island in the sea-eee
I've got,
a little wooden hut for me-eee.'

On a shelf at the end of the shed, above a can of three-in-one oil and a kindling axe, a trowel and a hand-fork, there is a damp cardboard box; the caved-in top has a picture of a railway station, a green steam engine making clouds of white smoke, passengers standing on the platform, men in coats and hats, ladies with gloves and handbags. The glossy picture has rough white patches eaten into it, and silvery trails where some of the train and faces and hands and coats of its passengers have been eaten by snails. Inside, the box has dividers to hold carriages, an engine and tracks, and a few pieces are missing. There are two brown-and-cream passenger coaches with table lamps visible in the yellow-painted windows, one coal tender with painted coal, a goods wagon with grained sides made to look like wood. There is no locomotive—perhaps it's on somebody's shelf somewhere as an ornament.

The boy takes all the pieces out, clicks the sections of track together on the bench: nine corners and one straight piece. The only closed track he can make is a circle using eight of the corners, so he puts the two extra pieces back in the box as 'spares'. He connects the rolling stock together, using the loops and hooks on the end of each carriage, and pushes the train around the track. He stops to pick up passengers by the tin of screws, then some coal by the window. Off they go again; they go round, then round again and again. He sees how fast he can make it go by pushing it hard and letting go, but the dried-up axles bring it to a quick halt. Adding the two spare pieces of track, he makes a longer open-ended line, a big meandering wiggle that snakes its way from one end of the bench towards the other. The wiggle is more satisfying. A proper journey, a scenic route that goes somewhere from somewhere else.

He builds a landscape with stones from the garden and twigs stuck in bits of mud, has fantasies about getting an engine, building a little town. Matchboxes from the house and empty cigarette packets for buildings. A couple of toy cars from his bedroom join the village, a tow-truck, a rocket and a milk van. All the different scales don't bother him as they would an adult—any child knows that the more you look at things, the bigger they get, a fact of life that many adults forget: tiny things can fill a world! A small tractor and some plastic pigs, which are nearly as big as the carriages on the train. A town grows at one end of the wavy line, and the country at the other. Of course there comes the inevitable wreck. The game does not last. He doesn't know what to do with these things, what they are for; the game can last only long enough to build the little bits of landscape. 'If I am going to drive a train, I am going to drive a real one, not push this fake one up and down,' he thinks. It was the game of an hour or so and then he neatly stacked the toys, the tracks and trucks and rolling stock and pigs, back in the box and returned them to the shelf, where they remained.

When he was twenty-one and drove a real train, did he remember this toy train then? I don't think so, but how can I tell? I can sometimes remember a thing, in a rough kind of way, if I really try, but can I remember remembering a thing? All our strands of memory are put away in order, like fairy lights, neat and tidy. There is only one way they can be 'in order' and an infinite number of ways they can be messed up, and just like this, a memory comes out tangled. But he did drive a train up and down the shunting yard. He wasn't supposed to, as it wasn't his job, but it was past two in the morning, the driver was drunk and crying in the mess hut and, like a good working-class man, he helped his buddy out by doing his job for him. If the driver's wife hadn't left him and he hadn't got sad, the boy might never have driven a train.

Beneath the bench there is a solid box, covered in dust, grey cobweb stuff and a few dead woodlice. An unusual kind of cardboard box, it once was blue with metal corners and rivets to hold it together; a lid, also with rusty rivets, is jammed on the top. It had been sealed with sticky tape that has lost its sticky and now lies rolled like an empty snake-skin, a crispy yellow coil on the boards. A symbol of luck, wealth, knowledge. The box is heavy. He has to sit on the floor to drag it out, searches for a grip and finally manages to get a few fingers under the edge of the lid and pulls. Four heaves gets it out of the shadows enough to prize off the top and release a scent that will remain with him for the rest of his life. He was expecting to find more rusty old tools, but in the dim light that crawls though the window and lands on the floor of the shed, gold glitters up at him.

From the darkness, Roman numerals, incomplete words:

IV Duo–Fun
V Fun–Hug
VI Hug–Lyr

These odd conjunctions glimmer against a dark-blue sheen. It is a collection of books, thirteen of them. An encyclopaedia, the blue covers spotted with grey mould; the top edges of the books are gold, and the lettering on the spines and covers is gold, and gold is gold for ever, so they shine through the patina of dirt with a beautiful glow. He has found a treasure on his island. These are his first books. The first of possibly thousands of books. Volumes 10 and 11 are missing—there should be fifteen if the set were complete. An incomplete train set, an incomplete encyclopaedia.

He hauls out one of the heavy books and leans into the pages. Having been closed perhaps for decades, it releases that old-book musk, a perfume that will forever excite his mind. He tumbles into big yellowing pages, dark pictures and tiny words imprinted, indented by inked metal type from noisy oily presses that cranked them into the world. Over the hours these thin old leaves, yellow and slightly damp, show him a universe of things outside his house and family and garden. They give and give and endlessly give, and he takes in the world's weather systems and the water cycle; how copper is mined; what a Bessemer converter is; the coffee that comes from a bean on a tree in Brazil; the rubber for the smelly beige soles of his black canvas gym shoes, which was bled from trees by semi-naked 'natives' who cut neat parallel rows of diagonal grooves into their bark with hooked knives, letting the sap roll down and drip the trees' white essence into little cups tied to the trunks with vines; then men sit on the dusty earth and roll it into balls by hand and send it in bales to factories in cities, where it's made into shoe soles and tennis balls and tyres for buses and waterproof coats and a million other things. Tea that comes from China and India—he examines the pictures of women in long flowery dresses with massive baskets hanging on their backs from straps over their heads, some with babies tied with sheets to their fronts as they bent and picked the top two leaves from bushes of *Camellia sinensis* growing in rows on a steep rainy hillside.

He absorbs the spotty black engravings and damp grey photographs of the 'peoples of the world': women with plates in their mouths making their lower lip hang out, posing for a camera; women with tall stacks of metal rings around their necks looking down from their height, stretched so long in the name of beauty that if the rings were removed, the women would die. He devours the

images of Maori men with fierce eyes and curlicues tattooed on their chins with needles of wood and little wooden
hammers; tall black men and women carrying spears and
showing their breasts, small children peering from behind
their hips; fully grown men as small as children, who use
blowpipes and poison darts to hunt monkeys and birds for
food; mud huts, houses on stilts; men sitting on poles in
the sea and fishing with rods; a row of men hanging from
a gallows with their necks strangely elongated, like the
women with the rings (he flicks back and forth between
these two images); girls in grass skirts smiling at the camera, with men looking on suspiciously from behind them.

The boy doesn't mind at all that some of the volumes
are missing—he did not know that such a thing could exist
and surely no set of books could have everything in the
world in it, so the missing volumes don't bother him too
much. Why obsess about what he does not have? He has
these treasures, which he hasn't had before, and maps of all
the world, and the index that shows him what was in those
missing volumes, so life is good and he can set out on an
adventure, exploring the recorded world of everything that
doesn't begin with the letters from New to Ros.

He sits on the stool with his pile of old books on the
bench in front of him. In the corner, a candle found in a
kitchen drawer; he has set it on a flat stone and decorated
around it with snail shells and stones and flowers, and pine
cones and seeds and a twig in the shape of a man, and a
bird skull and a plastic motorbike because he wants to have
a motorbike one day. It is a hearth, a heart, a sign of being

home, an altar, a symbol of his occupation of and partner-ship with this place—his place of power, his light in the darkness.

The boy's house had very few other books: some old cowboy stories that his father kept lined up on a shelf, some romances in his parents' bedroom, about seven books in total. Reading was not a thing to be caught doing, unless you were seriously ill. If he sat down to read at home the Angry Dog would growl.

'Haven't you got anything better to do?'

After a few unpleasant early interactions, he realised that such statements were not actual questions requiring a truthful answer, but instructions to find a useful task the Dog approved of, or just to 'go away'. Why can't people simply say what they mean?

The boy had been banned from the school library; he had taken some books back that were overdue because he had missed some school, and 'to teach him a lesson' his father had refused to pay the fine, so the school librarian had told him that he could not take any more books out until the fine had been paid. He could go in the library at lunchtime to read, but every time he looked up she was watching him as if he was up to no good, so he stopped going. It was a shame really because he liked her face; she was interesting to look at, although she didn't smile, she had pale hair and round glasses, and her face was covered with spots that sometimes seemed sore and weeping, and she wore long dark dresses with flowers on them. She obvi-ously didn't like him, but he liked her and thought she was pretty, so he looked at her a lot, and she was always watching him. At night he imagined her arms around him and her kissing his cheek, and the cool feel of her long flower-print dress against his skin and her legs through the cotton—he thought that would feel nice.

WHEN THE BOY was sixteen he went wandering across the countryside, sleeping at the edge of the fields like a hedgehog, by rivers like a water sprite, in woodlands like a fox. Having nowhere to live, he had decided to go on an adventure and he came across some hippies sitting round a fire—people who, like him, refused to take part in the violence and hatred of the world and didn't trust those who enjoyed power. They were playing guitars and singing; he curled up to sleep at the edge of the field they camped in, and a girl with long brown hair, who reminded him of that librarian, climbed under his blanket.

'What's your name?' she asked, and he told her the name he'd been given as a baby. Spooned together, she whispered into his neck, sending a shiver down his back, 'You should be called Spring Rain, or Autumn Cornstalk.'

That is why I call him 'Rain' in this story. We should all be able to change our names whenever we feel like it, to honour our fluid nature and so that we are not pinned down into ways of being that are gone. The reason we don't is simply bureaucracy—people without governments who want to keep track of them change their names all the time.

Arranging flowers, skeleton birds, a broken shed and letting go

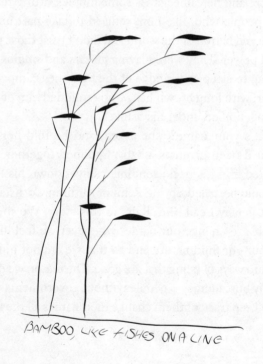

BAMBOO, LIKE FISHES ON A LINE

Evaporated water vapour rising from the warm earth meets the cold air, where it condenses into tiny drops that drift about in masses, making clouds. Their blanket covers everything with a feltiness right now. As the tiny droplets wander in their clouds they bump into each other and, being sociable, they join together. Together they are heavier and fall. According to the Met Office, if the droplets that fall are smaller than 0.5 mm in diameter they are classed as drizzle. Rain itself is described in three ways:

1. Light rain falls between 0.01 and 0.1 inches per hour.
2. Moderate rain falls between 0.1 and 0.3 inches per hour.
3. Heavy rain is anything above 0.3 inches per hour.

It is sad that the people who know about rain have no better descriptions than these.

A 'light rain' falls on this concourse outside the railway station. I can hear Peggy's footsteps amplified by the tiny slap of shoe sole meeting wetness on the stone. The rain may be 'light' but she walks quickly, making a wake through the air and dispersing the clean wet smell. I recognise her tread and turn to see her coming, huddled down. She hasn't brought her umbrella so she snuggles under mine; her warm left arm clamps around my waist and she kisses me a damp, cold kiss that lands clumsily on the cheek because our arms are full, and her face is wet and we are walking and I am tall and she is not. I hold my brolly over her and my left side gets soaked to the skin as we walk.

On the way to the bus, through the glistening drops that catch the lights from the cars and the shops, I carry her bag and she carries the flowers and says, 'They're lovely; they'll get damaged, though, on the way home.' Then she looks at my tie and starts to laugh; and I feel offended but laugh it off.

'I thought it was fun . . . I think it suits me,' I say.

'It does. I like it, it suits you,' and so on. 'I'm not laughing at your bow tie, I'm laughing because you have your jumper on inside out.'

'Oh.' I roll my eyes. 'I thought it felt funny.' I say, 'It must have been like that all day.'

I feel foolish but try to hide it, but Peggy knows and smiles and says, 'You look lovely—really you do.'

We watch through the tear-streaked glass of the bus, and the vehicles splash on shiny tarmac, smudged by the rain; the childishly bright wax-crayon-coloured cars and vans move and queue like chunky plastic toys designed for toddlers' unformed minds and hands. The colours bright, the shadows deep and detailed. Passers-by with bright umbrellas, which would in sunlight seem as gaudy as a carousel, emerge from shade and look as dignified and elegant as peonies, and all the passing colours seem as soft as fish in a pond or pastel jellyfish bobbing along. Everything is on hold.

We leave the bus and wander, dripping down the street with our broken flowers. Animals take shelter; pairs of jackdaws climb in covered chimney pots, the street cats curl up under cars or sneak into sheds. Sparrows cheep in the bushes; a black fly hangs under a rose leaf, upside down while the drips roll off to the earth. Underneath the cherry tree at the end of the path a cat that I call 'eyes too close together' shelters by a crust and looks nonchalantly into the tree, where a fat magpie looks down. We watch the magpie drop and the cat leap, and we cheer as the bird flies off with the crust; the cat looks embarrassed, then licks a back paw as if it never had any intention of catching the magpie anyway and was only pretending.

At home we hang our jackets up, take off wet shoes and I change into blue tartan pyjamas, and Peggy runs a bath. While I hear her splashing about and showering her hair, I cut the flowers from their cone of bronze paper and cellophane, which is closed with Sellotape and difficult to open. With the kitchen scissors I snip two inches off the stems at a steep angle and arrange the orange and yellow flowers in a clear glass vase on the kitchen table. They are gaudy and unsuited to the white room, but looked good in the cloudy street when I bought them. They would be better on my desk in the shady corner. The bright-green stems have tiny hairs that catch silvery bubbles that glow in the water, and perhaps the way the water bends the stems and magnifies and clarifies intrigues me the most: water the cleanser, the bringer and remover of life.

I like arranging flowers, it is a simple art that turns out to be not so simple at all. Creating a satisfying, asymmetric display that looks naturally unbalanced, as if they had fallen in that way or grown and been leaned on by wind and rain and had emerged just so. I light a candle next to them, to sparkle through the plain glass vase and make a flickering shadow on the wall.

I used to grow flowers, prune roses and cut lawns in a rich old lady's garden for a living. The years went by and the trees that I planted as sticks bore fruit. For a few years I collected the apples and raspberries for her, and she crushed or boiled them into cider and jam; and in later years her interests changed and the fruits fell to the earth and lay there fermenting, smelling lovely and boozy in the sun, intoxicating wasps, until I took them to the compost heap. Flowers aged and spread too much or died, and I dug them out and composted them, split them into smaller clumps or replaced them with new ones; and I came to know two toads, three foxes and several cats, some robins and some crows as individuals. As they grew older, the foxes and cats passed and I buried the bones that I found below the trees I had planted, which marked their territory, and their children circled and sniffed around, apart from the crows, which—like the toads—just disappeared. I imagine skeleton birds in the trees and toad bones still squatting in the stone-wall gaps where they lived. A gardener learns not to grasp onto changing things, but to let go and embrace whatever happens next.

My body can't do that kind of work any more, but my mind is all garden: constant bloom and seed and bloom. Gardening all day every day is hard physical work and, as I grew old and my body more worn, I would come home and drop heavily onto the sofa with my work clothes still on, and smelling of grass and earth and lavender or compost, and close my heavy eyes, too tired to change or shower. Peggy says that she knew I couldn't go on much longer. One day I was kneeling, pulling weeds from between the raspberry canes, and my knees made a snap when I tried to get up, a horrible popping feeling, and I had to crawl to the end of the row and pull myself to my feet with a post that I had hammered in there years ago, to carry the wires that hold the spindly raspberries up. The old lady I worked for watched me through her kitchen window. I felt like crying because I was embarrassed, and also because I knew it was the end and didn't know how I would buy food and pay my bills. From that point on, I needed a stick to walk with sometimes and stopped kneeling down so much. I used to like kneeling in the garden—it felt like bowing to the world that made me. Then, just a couple of months later, the lady died, and I closed and locked the gates and went home for the last time, put away the secateurs and mowers and peeled the signs from the side of my van. I still drive that van, but it's clean now and doesn't have tools in it any more, doesn't smell of earth.

Peggy says that I look healthier these days. I wake early, after years of getting up for work, and meditate for an hour or more, usually at dawn. It's not a discipline or a practice, I have no goal or aim, there is no ultimate purpose. It is something I do for the sake of doing it. I used to meditate a couple of times a week, but gardening was usually meditation enough. I do it nearly every day now. My relationship with the living earth seems distant since I left my job, and sitting silently feels like my truest nature.

I sit at the back door on a cushion, upright and firm like a tree; and, like a tree, I feel the dawn break and hear the first birds. I begin by feeling my breath: each single breath becomes the most vital, most wonderful living thing in the world as it arises like life itself, then leaves, and slowly I watch my thoughts float by and fade away to nothing, and I simply become aware and filled with peace. A rock in a stream. I feel the air flow in and out until there is no in or out; the birds pass by, the moving sun warms my skin— doing nothing, thinking nothing, being everything that is. You don't become nothing when you meditate; we talk of emptiness but it isn't really that. Words can't explain it, they are a human invention and trying to explain the infinite with them doesn't work. Some people talk of our everyday being as using our 'little mind', and of meditation as letting go of that and joining the 'universal mind'. It's like I wrote in another book: the sound of everything at once is silence, the colour of everything at once is white— in meditation, the world becomes silent and white and full of everything.

When I raise my eyes later I feel that I have added some peace into the world. Too much passive meditation makes me detached so much from everyday things that nothing and something start to feel the same. I could starve myself to death in that blissful state. The time to fade permanently into that kind of existence will come, but it isn't now, and that thought gives me freedom. I can walk and cook and eat and work in a state that is similar—mindful, but not the same, not as deep. It is good to be mindful; garden- ing creates, builds and strengthens mindfulness. This is why monasteries, and places of worship and learning of all kinds, usually have a garden attached. A garden is always a place of worship, even if it is a really crappy one. You can tell what people worship, by looking at their gardens.

My job was hard, exhausting, sometimes painful, but my body became habituated to certain movements and knows them well; my arms know how to reach up into branches, my back knows how to dig and push a barrow full of muck, my legs know how to lift my body up a ladder, my limbs want to move and work while they still can, my lungs crave the cold dawn air, my mind needs the silence of a frosty morning in the meadow or the woodland where I ate my lunch. Gardening is in my muscle memory and occasionally, when I'm out walking, I see a stem that needs pruning and absent-mindedly reach for the secateurs that for years hung in a leather holster on my belt every day.

I'm thinking more about the boy at the moment, perhaps because I am letting go of the past and I want to start again. It is not in my nature to look back, but unusually I find myself doing it. He seems alive somewhere, travelling on seas that are sometimes rough, with his books, exploring plants and insects, and I pick out the ropes that tie our distant ships together—the web we wove. We share the same joy of looking, the freedom of being, the poetry of words, of air, of movement. I want to tell you about him, I want to retell his story before I let him go, like all the other anchoring thoughts.

The neighbour's cat comes to visit while I'm still sitting, runs in from behind the log pile, rubs against my legs, back and forth a few times, then leaps on my lap, curls and spirals around like a snail and stamps and plucks, leaving ginger hairs on my brown corduroy trousers, and settles into the bed he has made. By the time he has relaxed I am ready to get up, but there is a natural law that states you cannot move when a cat is on you—it's a reminder from the universe that you have no real need to do anything other than stay exactly where you are, and the world will be okay.

I AM CAT-BOUND, cross-legged, anchored to my cushion. At the bottom of the garden my old shed is broken; it lies brown and dripping wet, listing like a washed-up hulk on the foreshore, its sides diagonal, but not quite at the point where the whole structure will fall down on its own—it needs a little push; perhaps the roses hold it up. The windows are cracked and the door hangs open, the rectangular holes they used to neatly occupy having evolved into trapezoids on their slow way back to earth. Roses clamber across the leaking clinker-built walls and roof and grasp it tight, hold and pull it inwards on itself—oh, how they flower! I planted them so many years ago for Peggy, who loves yellow roses. They flower like mad and their stems have grown knobbly and tough, to withstand the movement of the wind as they grind the shed to dust with their heavy arms and claws. Bindweed snakes in through the broken glass. A neighbour's tree fell on the shed in the storms, two winters ago, and cracked it like a walnut shell, so now the damp gets in and the walls, roof, floor and all the things inside have begun to fall to bits. Parts of the floor have become earth already and are occupied by woodlice and worms, while in the corner hangs a paper-wasp nest that's been abandoned. The imperceptibly slowly moving shed—unstoppable like an iceberg—has crashed into the rotting fence, so now it too leans at a similar angle. Whenever the weather was fine, I'd be working to earn my keep in other people's gardens and so my own fell to ruin; the shoemaker's children always go barefoot.

The fence on the other side of the garden is good and solid and made by my tidy neighbour, while the one I own is derelict and weighed down with ivy, its legs rotted off where they always rot, where air and earth meet. A firethorn with a crop of ripe sparrows that sing in the rain. They forget I'm here and cease to hide. Blue tits flit in and off the lilac tree. Next door's bamboo leaves, tethered to their stems, flutter like fish on a line.

Alburnum
to Chamomile

In his shed the boy arranges the volumes of the encyclopaedia in order and opens volume I, A–Beo; he flicks through
it, looking at the black-and-white illustrations: Alexander
the Great, Allspice, Ape, Aphides, Ark of the Covenant,
Armadillo, Arrowroot, Artesian Well. He stops at a two-
page spread with drawings of Aircraft; the caption says in
capitals MODERN TYPES OF AIRCRAFT and he reads the
names, written in friendly italic handwriting below them:
France—Amiot Multi-Seat Fighter, Germany—Junkers
Monoplane, Italy—Fiat Cabin Monoplane, Britain—Bris-
tol Two-Seater Biplane, and many more aeroplanes that do
not look anything like the Vulcan bombers that carry live
nuclear warheads over his house nearly every day, or the
massive planes dropping Agent Orange that he sees on TV
every night.

The facing page has a drawing of the Graf Zeppelin and he flicks to the front of the book to find the words 'Copyright 1933' in plain type on the centre of a page of its own, and a flicker of disappointment as he wonders if he should reject it as old and useless. Flicking back, an engraving catches his eye. A section of a tree trunk under the heading 'Alburnum'. The rings of the log are labelled in italic script: d—a—b—c—b—a—d. Then, underneath, a key: a—Alburnum or sapwood, b—Heartwood, c—Pith, d—Bark. He reads these words in a whisper to himself, 'Albernum or sapwood, Heartwood, Pith, Bark.' Then, looking at the diagram, he organises them in the correct order, from the outside to the middle: Bark—Alburnum—Heartwood—Pith; and whispers them to himself over and over again, imagining the damson tree over his shed sliced open and seeing its Bark, Alburnum, Heartwood and Pith. Then again, from the middle outwards, until he can chant it easily either way. He looks at the walls of the shed he is inside, the grain along the planks of wood that, from the ends, form part of a circle of tree trunk that grew once with other trees, had leaves or needles, birds, insects and maybe squirrels in its branches, made from Bark, Alburnum, Heartwood and Pith. Unlike the train, the shed is a real thing, a hut made of real wood, and somehow this seems significant, but he's not sure why.

He softly chants and commits the sequence to memory, while his eyes fall on the open pages on the floor in front of him, to catch the words: ALBION METAL, AL'BITE and ALBUMEN. The first three letters are the same and he turns the pages back to the first appearance of ALB and

39

reads that it means 'white', and he tracks the progress of Alb through Albany and Albatross and Albino and Album and Albumen, and masses of other things beginning with Alb that are white.

The boy feels that a world of excitement, of knowledge and curiosity, is here. A ripple of magic—things that appear very different from each other are connected. Each time he thinks of the books for the next few days the wave of excitement returns. This is just two pages, and the book has 600 pages, there are twelve volumes. He doesn't do the maths, as he is not good with numbers. He wonders how to use this wonderfully poetic thing. All these things. All these millions of wonderful things. Is it a book to read from Aahhotep to Zygote or one to jump in anywhere? He skims the first two volumes, stops from time to time to read about Birch and Bird of Paradise, Bivalves, Blood, Buttercups and Buttresses, Camera Lucida and Camera Obscura, Capillaries, Cave Dwellers and Chamomile. And he becomes full of hope and wonder at the complexity and connectedness of all the marvellous things of the world.

While he reads and devours the drawings, the rain stops plopping on the wooden roof, and the sun pushes apart the clouds, which break into small jigsaw pieces and drift away. He moves to sit in the doorway, with his feet on the wet step below. The world begins to steam itself dry; a bird sings with notes and trills and ups and downs and wobbly bits, from inside the holly tree. In the bushes the sparrows chatter and there's the smell of wet leaves, wet grass, the warm oily wood of the shed, damp stone drying in the sun.

He feels a bit damp and a bit warm and a bit lovely, as if he should be a gnome in the garden just being there, staying like this for ever with all the other things that belong there, until moss grows on him and snow settles and frost crystals develop and his paint peels off in the weather.

He steps outside and spreads his arms to the sun. He is filled so full of love and wants the animals to come to him, the birds—the blackbird and the magpie and the crows and the wood pigeons—to land on him, and especially the robin. He wants them to feel safe because he would not hurt them, and it occurs to him that he has been eating animals as if they were food, and he decides that he isn't going to eat the birds any more, or the cows or the pigs or any of the animals, come to that. Anything that has eyes, he decides. Anything that can see somebody coming after it. Anything that might feel afraid. The boy knows what fear feels like and doesn't want to pass it on.

He announces his decision not to eat the animals. He tells his mother first, who says: 'Oh, for God's sake!' Then a moment later she turns to look at him and says in a heart-felt, fearful way, 'Do not, for Christ's sake, tell your father.'

But he tells the Angry Dog anyway for these reasons:

1. He is proud of his decision.
2. He is feeling rebellious (sometimes being in trouble is better than being ignored).
3. The Dog will notice at some point anyway.
4. If he is going to get punished, it would be best to get it over with.

5. He is not afraid.
6. If he gets punished, it will be to save the animals.
7. He hates the Angry Dog and wants to cause him pain.

Nothing we do in life ever has only one reason; we usually do what we were always going to do, then we find as many reasons as we can to try to explain or justify what we have done.

'I'm not going to eat the animals any more,' he says.

For some reason the Angry Dog is not so angry and he merely says, 'Fine, all the more for us then.' And then, 'What will you eat?'

'Just the vegetables.'

'Fine, off you go.' And that is all he says.

The boy feels a tiny sense of anticlimax, as if he wanted to see his father angry, to make his decision more real and permanent and powerful. But also he's coming to see that the Angry Dog is unhappy, and he wants to make him unhappier. We carry our anger, our own irritation, like a hot coal—it hurts us far more than the person or thing we are angry with. Children are not powerless, they can make susceptible adults feel guilt, or anger, or protective; they learn quickly about people's triggers and enjoy pulling them; they don't have a lot of power, but they enjoy the little they have.

Over the weeks he scrapes clean and oils the secateurs and the hammer; the pliers' hinge was rusted hard, and they broke when he tried to loosen them by hitting them with the back of the axe (the little hammer was too light). The axe went from rusty red to polished brown over the months that he used it to chop kindling helpfully for the coal fire in the house. He used the secateurs to cut branches to sharpen with his penknife, but the secateurs were stiff and the hinge that joined the halves together had not been oiled for years, unlubricated and neglected; like a couple careless of what joins them together, the handles separated from each other in his hand. He left the box of seeds in the drawer.

GARDENER

Venus, Lucifer, jellyfish, sunshine, crackly voice

It is early spring and still quite cold, but the daybreak is friendly and does not disturb me too early. I sleep with the blinds open, so I can watch it arrive. A tiny spider crawls up the bedroom window, merging with each slat of the blind, then appearing again, until at last it lodges in the corner. I'm lying on my side, my left eye closed and buried in the pillow; my right eye sees through the glass, through the atmosphere of Earth, through thirty-eight million miles of space to bright Venus to the west, the morning and evening star. Venus is also known as Aphrodite, spirit of gardens, goddess of love, and is associated with heaven's most beautiful angel, Lucifer, 'the bringer of light' who, thrown down by his God because of his pride, was chained to a fiery lake. On Venus it rains sulphuric acid, and the snows that fall on the mountain tops are molten metal.

There are planets and stars above, and Gods of all kinds, if you have them; and there's us and the flowers and hills below, and in between there's gas and creatures and tiny bits of stuff. Over the silhouetted hill of Peggy, and her snowfall of white bedclothes, the Milky Way is cast like seed across the blackness. The heating struggles against the deep cold, so I pull my shirt over my head and wrap a towel around my waist and go downstairs to make hot chocolate. I like the cold on my bare feet, I think it is because I am tall and have always had to have my feet poking out from the bottom of the bed in the cold, so I have got used to it; if my feet are warm I am uncomfortable. While I wait for the kettle to boil I open the kitchen door and look out on the glowing pinkness of sky. There are an infinite number of ways to live a beautiful life and this simple one is mine: quietly, peacefully and with love. Each new moment, if I care to look, I'm presented with opportunities to turn my life this way or that, but I'm reminded of the one and only final destination as my knees click in the cold.

With a mug of hot chocolate warming my hands, I sit and wrap myself in a blanket while the light comes up behind the houses and makes the gas and tiny bits of stuff turn pink. For a while the day seems stuck in a fizzy, static state. I remember standing at dusk on a beach where I was to spend the night. I was homeless then and wandered every day. I had no destination—just wandering. You don't need to do an awful lot to have an adventure, you simply have to go outside your front door and start walking. Sometimes I would tramp to the sea, and sometimes I would go to the woods or find a river. I usually avoided towns and other people, but now and then I would go into a town to find a job for a while. This time I was at the sea and it was alight with pastel yellows and pinks and blues as millions of jellyfish congregated to fill the water with milky eggs and sperm. They merge and form polyps that sink to the bottom, and then grow and bud and make new jellyfish that will swarm in their turn when the weather is right and light up the sea again, for others to see. Some jellyfish can become polyps again and are considered immortal. A few years ago I met a man at a book festival, a yachtsman called David who studied animal navigation; he was a nice man, who came from a completely different world from me. He told me about a species of jellyfish that lives in a swamp and has twenty-four eyes that all look up to watch the stars, as mine do now.

The image fades and rain returns, which falls straight down like rice grains. How many dawns have I witnessed—each as beautiful as the last—ten thousand? Silver, blue-grey sky, with a barely-there touch of rusty orange. The rain is always different and seems old today somehow, grey and lustrous: pewter, lead, familiarly human. Silver blue-grey and smooth. I'm cocooned secure inside my house and feel wrapped in soft tissue paper, as if I were a delicate vase bought from a prim lady in a department store—transformed and hidden and protected, in a fragile world made from thin sheets of pure tender. It is good to have a house; a day does not pass without me thinking, 'I love having a house.' It is a nice house, tall and white, it has three floors and big windows and looks over trees. All the other houses in the street are the same; it's a cul-de-sac and the tall houses lean against each other like books on a shelf, each with their own stories inside.

One half of the sky is still bruised and yellow like a blackened eye, but just over there is a patch of blue that's clear and bright. Gently the greyness eases and a bright sun takes away the mysteries. The poplars sway, and crows and flies and people and their cats and dogs come out and catch the breeze and flap about like dancers or bed sheets on a line. Released from the closed-in private place behind the veil, the rain has passed; with the spell unmade, we re-join the world to go about our business. I need to make this broken garden whole again, as it's not a useful space any more, it is something left over—a museum, a mausoleum that needs to change so that I can change too.

Peggy stirs upstairs in her nest and I call, as I always do, 'Is that you, my queen? Are you awake?' I can hear the smile in her sleepy voice as she answers in a lazy stretching, 'Ye-e-es.'

'Are you ready for a cuppa?' I ask.

'Yes, please,' she says, so I make her some tea in her white builder's mug and myself some coffee, and take both mugs back to bed, where we cuddle and chat. Every single day begins like this. Everything else about the day often changes, but this routine, it's fixed. Peggy lies with her head on my chest, my arm over her shoulder, her naked body close to me. Quietly I sing an old song to her, 'You are my sunshine'; she is my sunshine, my only sunshine, and as I sing that she makes me happy, she snuggles closer and softens, and I notice for the very first time that my voice has become crackly.

There are two kinds of old people. There are the old people who are in pain and miserable, and there are the old people who are in pain but who are light-hearted. All the old people are in pain. Only some of us have the skills to be able to laugh at it every day. Life is ridiculous and full of pain, and to be kind and happy is the finest act of rebellion I can imagine. Lasting happiness is a skill; it's not an easy skill to learn, but once you've had a glimmer of it, it is impossible to ignore. To get it, I gave things up; stopped competing against others, accepted nature's flow, handed myself to simplicity, accepted inevitability, change and meaninglessness, but most of all I had to forgive people. Time passes, things happen, nobody knows why.

It is easy to forgive people if you love them—that is one of the ways you know that you love them. It is often easier to forgive other people than it is to forgive yourself, but you have to do both. It's harder to forgive people you don't love, and even harder to forgive those who are greedy or selfish, violent hate-filled people who like to make you hurt, and those who want to count the things they have and compare them with the things that other people have. You can't change the world by changing other people. You have to start with yourself by examining who you are, the harm you do, the things you think and feel and say, the things you use and consume. You must forgive and begin each day from where you are today, with nothing left from yesterday.

I treat the whole world as if I were just visiting. I'm a guest in a place that isn't mine, I won't be here for ever and, like any guest, I don't always understand what's going on. I don't have to; sometimes I figure it out and sometimes not—it doesn't seem to matter either way. I am a guest and the only responsibility a guest has is to be polite and kind and generous, to stand against injustice and to offer to help honestly when you can. My views are not very fashionable.

FOR MY BIRTHDAY I was given a weather station. I set it in my garden, put it on a pole to catch the rain and wind. On the top, an anemometer: three cups that catch the wind and spin to gather data on the speed at which it blows. Below, a little vane that points to where the wind came from. The other tilting mechanisms, collectors and sensors are hidden inside a plastic shell the colour of a wet sky: '18 per cent grey,' a photographer would say, or 'Pantone Cool Gray 10 C' for designers. It tells me grey things:

The rain that fell last night was light.
0.5 mm of precipitation collected in four hours.
The wind force is two from the south, at 2 m/sec.
The temperature is 14°C.

It also tells me barometric pressure, the moisture content of the air and the temperature indoors and out. All it can do is numbers—this ugly lump of plastic that will be on the Earth for ever really disappoints; I wanted poetry. In 2006 the world's oldest living creature was discovered, a clam that, at 507 years old, was killed by scientists who were trying to tell how old it was.

Some knowledge you need and some you don't. But poetry you always need. All knowledge is the carving up of things, separating the world into smaller and smaller chunks and comparing them to each other. If you break a bar magnet in half, the two ends that once were joined now repel each other. Where there is 'twoness' there is opposition, where there is 'oneness' there is peace. Our cutting little minds can't handle the great vast oneness, they can only manage little steps and breaking things apart to examine what they are.

Right now the digital display says the wind is blowing at 1.6 metres per second. It could, I imagine, be designed to tell me useful little steps like this:

1. The bitterest cold you know: stay in, or pop out for a moment, but only for urgent supplies.
2. Warmer, but wear layers—corduroy or something wool would be fine. Good walking weather.
3. Clear sky with blue so blue, and gold and reds and yellows; grandmothers will find it chilly, but young men won't.
4. Frustrating rain so small you can't decide—keep your umbrella up or take it down?
5. Grey and boring: stay in, go out (who cares, at least it's dry).
6. Rain—stay in.
7. Dry, but your brolly will turn inside out, your hat will blow away.

8. Sunny—babies will need a hat. A certain type will have their shirts off in the street; best to look the other way.

9. You'll want your sunblock and shades (remember to rub it in, so you don't look stupid when you're trying to look cool). Wear shorts if you dare (if your legs aren't too pale—or thin—or old and wrinkly) or linen (but you will sweat).

10. Stay indoors with the windows open, or you'll get cancer on your stupid bald head.

All I have to do now is look through the window at the analogue world outside. I used to need to decide if I could go to my gardening job or not and had three different weather-prediction apps on my phone. But now I can just watch the flow doing whatever it does today, I can enjoy the whole and don't need to figure it out or break it into little digestible morsels.

Horse farm, Antaeus, wolfsbane, a dying wasp

The boy, as all boys do, becomes obsessed by everything that falls into his grasp. His life is the garden, the plants, the insects and weather, his shed, his books. His two younger brothers are closer together in age and temperament; they play together, walk to school together and chatter. They like the warmth and company of each other's babble, and so he drifts away and thinks they are needy and babyish. He likes to be outside, washed with the moving air and exploring. Alone in his wooden shed, he feels free and safe from the casual violence and humiliations of home. His mother cries and the Angry Dog barks and his brothers play and chatter and run, and he reads in his shed where it's quiet.

A teacher at school one day asked each child in turn what they hoped the future held for them—they were to write an essay on it. The children answer in the usual way: 'I want to play football for Manchester United and have a big house', 'I want to be a nurse, like my mum, and look after sick children', 'I want to have a horse farm', and so on. None of the other children's answers appeal to him, they seem stiff and unyielding—how could they want to do just one thing? As the children answer, he wonders what would happen if they did not get the horse farm or the football job? Is that the end for them, would they be miserable for ever? He doesn't understand how they imagine they will even be alive that far in the future; he cannot picture himself living that long, to be twenty, or even fifteen. He has no idea what his answer might be and he panics a bit, trying to think of something to say, and hopes that something stupid doesn't come out again. When his turn arrives, the words that appear unexpectedly are: 'I don't really mind what happens to me.' He could have put it better but, because he gets things wrong sometimes, he feels ashamed of speaking up in class, so he uses sentences that are as short as possible. After a moment's pause, and looking at him intently, the teacher kindly says, 'In that case I think that you will have a very happy life', and the boy is pleased and decides that she knows best and that he will.

He wonders if the Angry Dog will kill him one day with a slap or a punch too hard. He's already partially deaf in one ear, from when he was slapped against the newel post at the bottom of the stairs. The boy imagines stabbing—stabbing or clouting him with a hammer while he is asleep—or putting poison in his bowl. He's planned his plea of self-defence already, just in case, and has practised swinging the axe into a stump, preparing for the Angry Dog's attack. He's played out all the scenarios; if he aimed for the neck, it might be too high, the Dog might dodge back and the blow would miss, and then the Dog would come in and attack before he could turn the axe and swing it back. Better to aim low, for the widest part of his body, and at worst take his arm off at the elbow, and at best open his stomach to the air so that his puddings spilled on the ground. The axe leans inside the shed door and the boy has practised reaching in and grabbing it without having to look. He sharpens it on the granite step so that the edge is clean and bright.

The Angry Dog enjoys life and relaxes when things feel good; he likes being stroked and petted and fed, and being told how clever and big and strong he is, and likes people agreeing with him when he growls at something bad. But bad things like noises and surprises, or anything unusual or different, or people doing things he doesn't approve of— being too happy or too sad, being in any way different from him—disturb his mind and he barks and leaps and growls. He often makes people cry. When people are afraid, they are capable of anything, and the Angry Dog is always afraid and so everyone else is scared of him.

SPRING SUN AND HEAT, three kinds of bees in the pink flowers of the currant bush, humming near and far—here, now here, now here. He watches a big fat one, black and with a rusty tail, dig down between two paving slabs and bury itself with bits of leaf.

54

The boy is lying on his stomach in the garden. The bottom of a lavender shrub becomes a forest and there, among the twisted roots, is a doorway to another world below; at which an ant appears—it wanders by and then another comes and, as the boy's pupils narrow to take in all the detail, he sees hundreds of them pouring in and out of a citadel, he imagines, below the heavy perfumed canopy. Some of them seem to stop and chat, like people in the streets, and others carry little white bundles in their jaws. Head down in the dirt, he tries to see the ants' world and what the ants might see, and his garden now seems far too big ever to fully understand it. He fears that he can never know everything of this vastness, and perhaps he has to choose to know as much as he can about one thing or two, or four; or, on the other hand, not choose any path or goal at all, but simply look at whatever grabs his attention. There might be just too much to know—it all seems far too big, and somehow that feels lovely.

He looks up 'Ant' in his books and learns that the little white bundles they hold in their jaws are babies, whom they bring out to enjoy the sun, like humans take their prams out to the park, then home again when it gets cold. He brings a few grains of sugar from the house for the ants, but then thinks that he shouldn't interfere, that it feels like involving himself in their lives is somehow wrong, that he could appear to be a God to them and they would come to rely on him and, when he went on to other things, they would not be able to cope. He doesn't want to be a God, does not want any power that would require him to feel superior; he wants to let the ants be themselves, be free of tyrants and live their own lives—he knows all about dependency and tyrants. How they whine and complain like babies: too hot, too cold, too much of this, not enough of that, this is unfair, they should do this, they should do that; they say 'should' an awful lot, and it's all about being in charge and making their own lives easier. So he leaves the ants alone, sits on his step and reads to them aloud: 'Ant. The common name of hy-men-op-ter-ous (or mem-bra-nous—winged) insects of various genera, of the family Form-ic-idae, of which there are numerous species.' He doesn't know how to pronounce these complex words or what they mean, and notes that later he really should remember to find the volumes that might tell him.

He reads to the ants as they go about their business. 'There are at least 2,000 species of you, and you are strong and social and clever, and sometimes you grow wings and have farms where you milk aphids and caterpillars as if they were cows, and you kidnap ants from other colonies and make them into slaves'.

The book moves on to the next topic, Antacid; he reads about Alkali for acidity in the stomach (which is boring), then of Antaeus, a giant, son of Poseidon the sea, who was invincible so long as he was in contact with Gaia the Earth, who was his mother. Antaeus challenged all the strangers in his land to wrestle him and he beat them with his earthly strength, but Hercules figured out his weakness and lifted him off the ground, held him in the air and crushed him to death. Sitting on his step, the boy imagines being Antaeus, how it would feel to be lifted from the ground, and the injustice and sheer bloody frustration of being held up by

56

someone stronger, unable to move, unable to touch the earth, powerless, like a child taken from his mother.

In volumes IV and VI of his books, marked Duo-Fun and Hug-Lyr, he explores 'Formicidae' and 'Hymenopterous', and on the way he finds out how his eye is built, and reads the labels on the diagram: AQUEOUS—CORNEA—LENS—VITREOUS—RETINA—FOVEA and HYALOID CANAL. Many diagrams show the muscles attaching the eye to the skull and rotating it, the tear ducts and the iris. Sitting on the dusty step surrounded by several open books and the sound of bees, there is no other place in the world that he would rather be, in contact with the breathing earth that makes him strong, and finding truth and wonder.

Darkness starts to fall and his mother is knocking on the kitchen window. As he closes the book he glimpses the illustrations of the eyes of frogs and limpets and squids and honey bees and snails and jellyfish. His mother's knocking continues, sounding irritated now, and he knows he has to put the books away, close the shed and set off to the house. He feels lifted from his earth, and his power and his freedom fade into a kind of death. He leaves the book open on his workbench and, unwilling to leave, he flicks through to where he sees a picture of an acorn and oak leaves, ready to read when he gets back. When he does, he will read on the same page about Aconite or Wolfsbane, also known as Monkshood. He will read that it is a deadly poison even in small doses—just touching it can make you ill. He reads that it's common in sunny gardens, and from the little engraving he will identify it growing in a little clump by the sunny wall.

A wasp dies slowly on its back by the door as he goes in, its legs winding down to a stop. The boy leans over to watch and, thinking that it's probably okay to interfere with nature by saving a life, but not entirely sure of this, he brings it syrup made in a teaspoon from sugar and water from the tap, and drops it near the wasp's dark head. He wants to see it fly again. He feels its life falling slowly away from its body, a wasp-shaped life somehow disconnected from its frosted-glass wings and crispy-looking flesh, and he feels saddened but honoured to witness this humble, ending thing and finds it oddly beautiful. Funny how a death is embarrassing; strange that it can be beautiful.

— 8 —

GARDENER

Ship of junk, memories, happiness, Thor

I LIKE FLOWERS ON MY DESK

59

The sun is daily creeping closer to the earth and I am in my shed, which, like a net behind a trawler, has caught the aggregated flotsam of old and broken things that wash around and never seem to leave. It's packed to the roof with history; with tools, paint and brushes, hard like hammers. A creature has chewed through the lid of a can of linseed oil and it lies on its side, its contents a brown jelly on the boards. Big tools with engines and wheels, a rotovator, a shredder, three lawnmowers tilt on the failing floor like loose cannon rolling across the deck of a sinking man-o'-war; about a hundred mole-traps hang like ammunition on a hook. On the bench there are clamps and drills, spanners and stones of different grits that are specially shaped for honing the blades of shears and scythes and secateurs. Artist's tools for carving stone and painting pictures, canvases, boxes of sketchbooks, notebooks reaching back for decades, collected, added to and hoarded, never abandoned although unused, as I wandered my days through various jobs and different ways of life, and abandoned those ways while keeping the stuff and the tools as if some day I might go back.

I will not go back. Returning or standing still is death and so, to make space for something new, I have to clear away the old and build something new, while I am still capable of using the memory that lives in my muscles before that memory fades. I want to return it to a natural state, that is reason enough; it is ugly for me, as a guest on this Earth, to mess up the bits I've been loaned.

My life now is much simpler, and the history of a life is an ever-shifting story told through objects and events. Nothing is fixed if we constantly learn, observe and grow, becoming more layered and subtle and fluid. Meanings and values change, points of view fade and shift, and life is ever flowing onwards. One should not try to dam up and contain the past. I love the stream and it should be allowed to flow in torrents and waves and not back up, to flood the present in stagnant, drowning water.

On a shelf a row of wooden box-files lean against each other; they are dusty and stuffed with history, mostly paperwork, garden designs and invoices, but also there are notebooks with my drawings, stories, poems, notes about how to temper steel, the names of the planets, the Demons and the Gods, the Angels associated with them, the melting points of lead and copper, silver, brass and gold. A page of colour charts from my watercolour box; a drawing of my son, aged somewhere round about seven, looking up at the sky; a faded Polaroid of my daughter, a naked toddler wearing painted cardboard wings that I made for her because she desperately wanted to fly. I don't know what to do with all this stuff.

'Look, Peggy,' I shout. 'Look at this photo—remember this?' And she comes and smiles at the chubby little girl, looking seriously at the camera and at her father the liar, who said he would make her some wings, which she believed would make her fly.

In memory there is always melancholy; even in the happiest memories there is a reminder that all things become yellow, like the backs of my hands, and turn to dust. Susan Sontag said that all photographs are memento mori—one-thirtieth of a second or thereabouts that is for ever lost, its ghost caught and held in crystals of blackened silver halides, trapped in a layer of gelatine on a piece of glossy paper. There is a natural melancholy about a photograph, more so than a drawing, which has more of a life; it takes time to make, the subject moving and growing as you draw it. I'm still driven to make some kind of art and when I read Sontag's comments, I started making photographs that captured this feeling deliberately and posting them on my website, photographing the flowers on my desk in black and white on my old film camera, developing it in the kitchen. Washing prints in the stainless-steel sink, I think of my mother in the steam that rose around her. A flower in black and white, a flower like all the rest of us, and while I think of her she is here—I stand behind and hold her, and she is smaller than me now.

Perhaps my own failings as a father sadden me a bit, that I could not make my little girl fly. I was terrified of being a father. For years I told myself that I would not allow it to happen, but nature finds a way. I am a selfish, solitary man who would rather sit alone on a cushion watching birds fly or a stream flow by than go to play football with friends. I have few friends; I have streams and wind and rocks and rain instead. What kind of a father could I be? Nobody taught me how to be a man or a father. At school one of my English teachers asked the children about their role models.

The boys named footballers and superheroes from comic books. I knew nothing about any of those things, and when my turn came I spurted out, 'Doris Day.' Why? Because in the old films that my mother loved she was clean and well loved, she was pretty and smiled, she was nice and funny and seemed to be able to care about things without screaming. I wanted to say Cary Grant, but could not for the life of me remember his name. My memory has never been good.

So, as a father, I suppose I channelled a mixture of Doris Day and Cary Grant. They were all I had to work with. When my son wanted me to play football, somehow Doris came out; in fact Doris came out more often than Cary, now that I come to think about it. I still know nothing about football, but I can waltz around the room for hours with a toddler in my arms and La-la-la at least three Strauss waltzes and sing the words to 'Sweet Little Buttercup'. My daughter enjoyed it. I think my son was less impressed, but they both learned to fly in different ways.

My children do not need the burden of my tat—they would probably be embarrassed by it. In the end I put aside a box-file and save a few images that will, pragmatically, stay in the box until they become someone else's problem; they'll laugh perhaps or smile sadly for a moment, then put them away and forget them and get on with their lives. The greatest thing Peggy and I can do for them now is to let them see us have fun together, to love each other and laugh until the end of our days. They don't need us now, they have their own lives, but we can show them by example how to love all the way to the end.

If I dug out all my memories and piled them on a scale, put the carefree in one pan and the gloomy in the other, the happy side would be piled high, overflowing and light and the darkest side would hold a tiny, denser lump, a little solid block of grim, yet that side would fall so hard and fast it would hit the ground with a mighty bang. There has been far more contentment, wonder and happiness in my life. But misery is dense, it is heavy, grey and leaden, and the lighter, fluffy peace and happiness would bounce right from the pan to float into the sky, to drift on the breeze through blue and joyful emptiness, while the melancholy would land in front of me and stink like a dead dog on the carpet, dragging my spirit down. As I sift through the memories and separate one from the other, evaluate and judge, the joyful fly and the sad ones lie. So I take another tack, decide not to slice my life into good and bad, not to measure or weigh or value in one way or another, but instead to mix them up again and let them be together as they should—both good and bad together make a life.

This melancholy, fed by a spontaneous vortex of feelings and thoughts, is a natural physical response. What you pay attention to in life gets bigger, and I could put some energy in and build the feelings up, but I let them go like swifts. I am left feeling complete and exhausted, after a flirtation with sadness that somehow feels wholesome, natural, ordinary, real. I prefer the peace and silence that follow.

When I look at the past I do it in the present, it becomes the present and I don't have any desire to cling to it. I make the three piles of stuff that we have all made at some time: a pile to keep, a pile to go, and a pile that I do not know what to do with. There is no better word to describe these things than 'stuff', accumulated like the fluff that rolls under the bed and needs to be swept away, the dust-bunnies my nana called 'slut's wool'. I gradually move it bit by bit, and everything eventually, after further examination, moves into the pile that has to go.

I advertise a bunch of tools and lawnmowers on the internet, and people come and take them away. I shake the hand of a grateful man who is starting his own gardening business. I tell him I used to be a gardener and help him lift the heavy professional lawnmowers into the back of his white pickup. They are his now. Walking back up the path as he drives away, I wonder why I said it: 'I used to be a gardener.' 'I used' and 'to be'. These tools created my identity, my 'being'. I think, 'He has my tools and identity now!' But of course it's merely a label describing a fragment of me—the fragment that most people knew. I feel a little hollow peace at letting go of that part, which is by morning replaced with lightness.

One day I'll be gone, and Peggy will have to deal with all the remaining things that bear my imprint: cameras and poetry books, old phones, trousers and watches, belts, cufflinks, wallet, glasses, notebooks, shirts and underwear, a shoebox of assorted bow ties. Would I go into that endless sleep and leave her wide awake, but tired and sad, with all my mess to tidy up before she can find any rest?

'I'm throwing away as much as I can,' I say. 'So you don't have to deal with it if I die' (if!).

'I'll cope, my love,' she says. 'That's years away most probably—most probably.'

'Build a bonfire and send it all to Valhalla, where I'll be waiting for my stuff?' I laugh and start to build a fire.

'Man loves fire,' she says in a caveman voice.

I imagine Peggy old and alone, and I'm driven to burn as much as I can and the bonfire grows. Bits of dead and crisping history sail by, like shed skin cells, and as it goes I feel lighter. Happiness is so much airier than sadness. The melancholy fades, the present finds its happy and begins to float, and I want to spend what's left of my life floating on it. Free and happy as a child, with no shackles or history to weigh him down. Stardust, golden.

The neighbour's cat rubs against my legs and leaves its ginger fur again. It comes through the pine trees at the end of next door's garden. I think it may be called Cyril, because often I can hear a man a few houses away calling, 'Cyril, Cyril' in a clipped voice, as if he knows Cyril is being unfaithful. Or is it Cybil?

I go inside, make a call, hire a skip and feel like a 'proper working-class man' who does proper manly things, like making calls and hiring skips, instead of the one I am, who sits by a fire, makes soup, drinks sherry, polishes his shoes, reads sonnets and writes them. The cat follows me in, then out again, and watches while I attack the empty shed with a crowbar. I open the gaps between walls and roof, then lift the sagging roof with my left hand and push the front wall in. The shed that once enclosed some space and dominated the garden, with its blocky darkness, folds gently,

66

elegantly in, like an old lady fainting and clutching at a side table as she slides slowly down, to prostrate on the ground. It leaves a ghost of where it has been, which will dissipate as I get used to the empty space, and the sparks from the fire fly high into the evening sky. Even the most seemingly permanent of objects are no more than passing events.

Over the next few days I smash the bits to smaller bits like Thor, with my rusty sledgehammer, and with a sense of joy make dust and space and emptiness. I remember, as a child, taking a clock apart to see what made it work and finding just springs and wheels and nothing else, no essence of clock. When we take things apart there is nothing; it is only their togetherness that makes them into something. Peggy and I heft the walls and roof of the shed through the house to the skip on the drive. We dump the remains of the shed on top of the junk that was inside it, and sweep the kitchen floor of bits that had fallen and were reluctant to leave.

Milder weather follows, and I clear the space until all that remains are the plants and trees and things I think I want to keep. I'm offered a pile of red bricks, so I drive in my van to collect them. I buy some massive bags of sand and gravel that are delivered on a lorry. Enough of each, I hope. I do not count or measure, and my guesses are often far more accurate than anything I might attempt to do with a piece of paper or a tape measure. I can, after all these years, comfortably accept that I am not that kind of man, but this kind—if there's not enough, I'll get some more; if there is too much, I'll give the rest away.

A knife, a feather, starfish and a magpie's tongue

wolfshane

His mother busies herself behind him, in her world. She hasn't spoken for what feels like an hour. She rarely seems to speak these days. She is draining the potatoes. He thinks perhaps he is like a starfish limb that has come off and wriggled away on little tube-legs and grown (while no one noticed) into a complete new starfish, whole and fresh. Who wandered off first; was it she who walked away from him? He was part of his mother perhaps, he doesn't remember that part, but is aware that now he is separate and he's never thought of that before.

Does she know what he thinks? Is she able to read his mind, hear his thoughts? Is what goes on inside his head completely private? He looks around to see if his mum has noticed what he's thinking. 'Can you hear me?' She doesn't turn. Her pale curled hair blends into the steam that twists from the potatoes, which she's poured with a rumble into a metal colander in the sink, and the scalding starchy water drains away. The bright window she faces is misted and sends soft light through her hair, through the steam, through her arms stretched down to her hands, which grasp the rounded stainless-steel edge.

He deliberately thinks, 'Turn around, Mum, and look at me.' But she doesn't, and he wonders, 'Is she ignoring me on purpose?'—another parental trick perhaps among so very many, as if she doesn't want him to be aware that she can know his thoughts, tries to keep this important knowledge from him. He needs a better test, so he thinks of a swear word he enjoys, one that makes him smile because it's rude: 'bugger'; and he sends the thought towards her, testing. Probing deep into her mind while watching closely, but still she doesn't turn or even flinch. More confident now, he bravely thinks the ultimate word—a word he's only ever heard, seen adults appear embarrassed at it being said while he was there, a word he'd never even utter—and pokes it hard towards her back, jabbing like a finger to her tender ribs, but still she doesn't turn. Instead she slowly mashes spuds with a hand-tool from the kitchen drawer while looking through the window. He thinks perhaps she is silently crying. Does she know? What does she know?

He still doesn't know if the newsreader on the television can see him, so when he gets undressed for bed and into his pyjamas, he goes behind the sofa. It has never occurred to him before that he is a separate thing, and it is both terrifying and exciting. He has said (or thought) a bad word and got away with it, and found that what happens in his head may very well be private. He's overwhelmed with a sense of freedom, or is it loneliness, or maybe fear? (Has he noticed yet that fear is fun?—perhaps not this time.) He wants to go and hold his mother from behind, but turns his thoughts away. This new idea is too big to process; he needs to give it time to ripen, for its fruits to become sweetly delicious.

He wants the safety of his thoughts and so he gazes through the window and slowly becomes lost, until he is drawn back by the smell and spattering sounds of frying sausages and the fuss of household bustle. He is told by his red-faced mother to put plates on the table, knives, forks, a bowl of peas, a bottle of tomato ketchup. He feels as if this new idea of separateness has cast a veil between him and every other living thing, and he is slow and vague and forgetful, careless, but manages to follow her instructions without accident. He is tired, he has had a busy day, so he sits behind his veil, alone between his father and his mother, and eats his mashed potato, peas and ketchup and wonders what can replace a sausage. When the meal is done and the plates are cleared, he's freed and wanders down the garden to his island, and leans like Prospero into his magic books.

He reads about wolfsbane in the open pages on his bench and goes to examine its lovely purple flowers, shaped like monks' hoods, in its sunny spot down by the wall. Two magpies chatter in the trees. 'Crark, crark,' he says back up at them. He looks up magpies in his book and reads that they are clever, crafty, robbers who steal shiny things and hide them. They are related to crows and can learn to imitate human words—'Just like the Angry Dog can,' he thinks, and smiles at his own mean corvid cleverness. On the way through the pages to find out about magpies he sees the word 'magic' and reads of the 'occult powers of nature' and of 'departed spirits' who can be 'summoned to do your bidding'. His grandmother from the Isle of Man is scared of ghosts and evil spirits; she says that magpies are witches in disguise and she greets them when they cross her path; she reads tea leaves and palms. He went looking for 'Occult', but the word was not explained in any of his books.

'Mum, what does Occult mean?' he asks her as she hangs out dishcloths—she who has been brought up by a cunning woman.

'Why?' she asks sharply. 'Why do you want to know this? Who have you been talking to?' she says in a panicky way.

'I just read it, Mum, and didn't know what it meant.'

'Where—where did you read it?' And he knows, from her reaction, that it is a dangerous or powerful word, a secret word that perhaps he should not know about.

'In my encyclopaedia—I was reading about magpies,' he says.

'Oh,' she says, relieved, 'some silly people think that magpies are magic, like your grandma thinks they're witches. Occult is another word for magic, but it's all rubbish.'

'Oh, okay,' he says and wanders back to his step, where he sits sharpening a stick with the old horn-handled pen-knife that his grandfather had secretly given him. A feather drifts down beside him as he chops at the stick, a gift from the witches above. He looks up and says, 'Thank you' and puts it in his hair, because he has read that Indian braves wore feathers to make them fearless, so he wears it and no longer fears the Angry Dog. As he carves he thinks, 'I am small and he is strong, but one day he will be old and weak, and I will still be young and strong, and then he'll see what it's like to be me.' The thought becomes a chant in his head and soon he finds himself whispering quietly, over and over:

'I am small and he is strong
One day he will be old and weak
And I will still be young and strong.

I am small and he is strong
One day he will be old and weak
And I will still be young and strong.'

Then the occult power of nature presents him with a second verse, just drops it in his head like a stone. It makes him smile; he almost laughs out loud and feels the world is a living, wonderful, beautiful, magical thing, with all the power he could ever need. 'Thank you, witches,' he looks up and says, before cutting at his stick and chanting his spell softly on his step:

'I am small and he is strong
One day he will be old and weak
And I will still be young and strong.

Oh, magpies with your cracking tongue
Who like to pick up shiny things
Come down and take his eyes.'

Outside the shed is a patch of earth that has a wall around it, three bricks high. At the far end there's a row of twigs stuck in the ground, which were there when he arrived, and climbing up and twisting around the twigs and clinging as they climb with fine and feathery tendrils there are peas. Perhaps they had fallen from last year's crop, which last year's gardener planted. Between them docks and dandelions grow, and groundsel with its little yellow flowers that never seem to open.

His mother asked with a smile if he had planted the peas. Her smile, that little smile, made him think of the seeds in the shed and, because of that smile, he wants to plant some more, so he gets on his knees and digs out everything but the peas with the hand-fork, and twists it into the earth to make the soil crumbly. He has never grown anything before, but the seed packets have instructions and he plants radishes in a row, like the packet says, and then lettuce and kale, each in a row of their own, and waters them in and thinks of how his mother will smile when he shows her his crop, and they will all eat it.

10

GARDENER

A new Eden, fear of the wild

✻ ❀ ✻ ❀

The garden whispers softly, like Ophelia driven mad with grief, and tells me how it would prefer to be. *Shhh, look! There's columbines here; plant foxgloves in the lilac shade for bees, and here plant ferns for their bright croziers and summer fronds, anemones for the wind, angelica and fennel for their frosted seeds and for the birds, and here put daisies and forget-me-nots for innocence, forgetfulness and uncomplicated love.*

It wants to fill my senses, be liberated, unconstrained, to make each mind that sees it feel slick and non-stick, so that whoever brings their fears, bad memories or worries here will lose them; they'll slide off and fall and crumple at their feet like autumn leaves, to rot and fade and leave them clean, washed and dusted, so they can be absorbed and swallowed in nature's wildness and its magic.

Any experienced solo hiker or country person knows the feeling of power that nature has when we silence ourselves. Go into the wild alone, away from human company or phone signals for a decent length of time—say, three days and nights—and the awareness of that power is inescapable, unavoidable, impossible to ignore. It can dominate your thoughts and take control of what you think, heighten your senses so that you feel it with your skin and hair, and steal you away into itself. Tiny sounds, tiny smells, tiny sensations will grab your unwilling flesh, push you around and tell you who you are. It is fearsome. Few people like to hike alone because of this. If you hike in a crowd and chatter, you drown nature out, but if you go alone you cannot fail to feel the energy that emanates, vibrates from every molecule of moving water, living cell and rock. There is magic in the wildness, in the mountains and the river valleys, and if you are silent you will feel its power.

There is a place I used to walk in from time to time, not a popular place—even to people in groups, it felt bad and dark and ancient. Noisy groups of hikers fell silent as they approached the rocky ridge where mountain ponies fed and sheltered against the Earth's grey bulging bones, which gnarled, twisted and jutted through the thin damp skin of tussocky grass and gorse, like the hill's own sleeping buried dragon. A place where you could easily imagine painted, mud- and gut-smeared Celts in wolf skins, building fires and roasting massive chunks of flesh at dusk, dripping into the spitting fire, sending glowing sparks high into the black sky; and witches being hanged or screaming while being burned; or sacrificing living things of skin and fur that howled and thrashed on the rocks as they were beaten dead and cut apart. You could smell the fat in the air, feel it on your skin. Casual walkers and locals took detours to avoid the place, apart from the odd one or two who, feeling their skin buzz with tension, kept their distance from each other and avoided eye contact. It is said that Iron Age kings were buried there, and French soldiers of the Légion noire. Even the farmer who owned it stayed away.

One would think that city streets would be haunted by the ghosts of the millions of souls who have lived and died there, but there's too much noise and energy and general busyness to feel their subtle presence. Be alone for an hour or two on that ridge, though, or in the trees of a forest river valley, and you will feel the presence of the force of life that you never will forget. You'll feel it in your bones and muscles and your nerve endings. Some will be afraid, while others will open up and take it in. From these real human feelings were born the tales of elves and trolls, sprites and demons. We like to tell stories because stories make us feel things, and feelings make us come alive.

Peggy grew up there by that hill, a little girl awash in this rich miasma; she started writing stories full of fear and dread and love and loss, and now she sits in the top of the house, three floors over my head, still writing. She cannot help herself—she is filled with it. I met her nearly forty years ago at art school, when our imaginations buzzed, and I fell in love with her magic.

Ornamental gardeners, fearing a chaotic earthly hell, have tried to tame the wild untidiness of nature, to eradicate it with organised precision in designs, and have planted museums of exotica collected and curated to impress. Anyone like me—any gardener, witch or druid, any worshipper of the earth who gets down on their knees, any earthy, grubbing labouring person with soil under their nails and dirty knees and peace deep in their mind—who knows that they are an offspring of the soil, an emanation of the earth, a vibration, they will see and feel and know, because it's as plain as day. No one else can feel it; if your nails are clean you cannot know, and you may even mock the ones who do, those oddballs with their muddy feet. Like Antaeus, we are strong while closely rooted in the earth that hums, and everything that we know springs from it wordlessly. Each of us is a living song that nature sings and, try as we might to overcome, we have no lasting power, we will not endure and it will sing its own infinite song. Solitary children who can hear it will forever look for fairies at the bottom of the garden, and be afraid of dark and hollow places where things bubble and rot in the stumps of old trees, because their fearful imaginations cannot help but tell stories to make sense of the terrible things that nature whispers in their ears, and the cloying, clinging smells that it wafts around their noses and sticks to their grubbing fingertips.

My house was built on ancient woodland. There are trees between all the houses, but more houses sprout up every year; yellow machines drag their teeth through the earth and chainsaws cut down the trees, and estates of red boxes with turfed gardens and decking spring up like fungus and cover the living land. We all have to live somewhere and I live here, so in my new garden I'll open a window to that underworld, cut a slit in the veil so that buried power can leak back into this ancient place. I want to see the living insects crawl and fly and lay, turn from egg to imago, and the birds that nest and eat them. I want to see and feel the life that thrives and fights in the soil and the air, and every inch will vibrate as if this ancient life is breathing under dusty bed sheets. There will be no sterile lawn to confound the bees and hoverflies, no concrete path to entomb the living earth, no vile, stinking wooden deck to starve the green and gather slime. There will be a simple narrow path of brick, no wider than it needs to be, that lets the rain and beetles through; and a place to put a chair or two, a shed for tools. The rest will live, with birds and fungus, rotting stumps, water, plants and shade.

THE SCENT OF wet and green and umber comes in and I gaze out at my tiny plot. The daffodils are open, rain taps the bricks and ferns and sage and brings the oily fragrance of mint to where I sit, by my back door in this tiny yard, in this row of yards, in this ancient town of small back yards, just outside my tall, thin house on the edge of town in a cul-de-sac of tall, thin houses built in 1972 while I was sleeping with hippies in a field. The garden measures sixteen paces from the back door to the fence at the bottom, and seven paces between the fences on either side. The bottom fence is twice as high as me, and the others half that size; I am six foot two. Other people's gardens surround it.

There are tall pine trees nearby that hide the sun from much of mine. This is the Rookwood: a few ancient trees remain, one or two lost every year to people who don't care enough for life that is other than their own. The man with the garden behind mine cut down the ancient copper beech and evicted owls and bats, and a trillion smaller things, because it dropped leaves into his plastic hot-tub. There was a tree preservation order on it, but that doesn't count for much round here. The hot-tub faded, cracked, then leaked within two years and was replaced with decking. The earth here wants to be woodland; it tries so hard, but gets cut back by people with tools powered by fuels made from ancient forests. I will free this patch again and make a place where sprites could come and feel at home—a portal.

The lilac is the largest thing here. I stuck a twig into the ground twenty-five years ago and it became a tree, and my children saw a tree grow. Trees want to grow here, dahlias do not. The lilac has a natural wildness in its twisted shape; it leans away from wind and folds towards the light as it makes the space its home. It grew twisted as it tried to reach the sun. Its shape tells the story of its life, just as our own shapes and features tell our stories. It's happy here, but its ancestors lived on warm breezy hillsides in Eastern Europe, and it can live for more than a hundred years. It flowers in spring and on a sunny day the perfume wafts into the kitchen. I intended to drink the wine this spring that I made from its flowers last year, but it was horrible and I poured it down the sink.

When you make a garden, you have to take into account the nature of the place. It's a mixture of the scientific and the romantic, with a massive element of chance mixed in.

I like to grow lavender—it's evergreen and smells delightful when you brush against it with a hand or passing leg; froghoppers bubble their spit in its branches, and bees on their way to make honey from its flowers will rest on you for a while as they pass. I've had two or three on my hand at a time, as I've snipped a few flowers off to tie in a bunch and take indoors. Lavender grows wild around the Mediterranean on hot, dry stony soil, but if you plant it in wet compost in the shade, it will die. Rhododendrons, on the other hand, come from the Himalayas, and many varieties grow in conifer forests where the needles fall and make the soil acidic and damp; if you put them in full sun where the soil is alkaline, the leaves will go yellow and they will die.

All living things will grow and thrive where they are happy, will struggle to survive where they are not, and will die if they cannot adapt to an environment that is hostile to their particular needs. Some species are more adaptable than others. Sometimes humans smash environments to smithereens and, from the dust, build new ones that did not exist before, but in doing this the species that are less adaptable—birds, tigers, dugongs, frogs—do not survive. A person's creative spirit is a living thing that needs the right environment too.

I will make a garden that is suited to the climate in this place. There's lots of shade, so it will be damp. I'll look for hardy plants that have a native woodland habit, ferns and broad leaves that catch the sounds of breeze. Ivies on the fence will feed the autumn bees. Simple single flowers will travel where they want to go and bring in insects and birdsong to announce the dawn and dusk; the drone of bees for warmth. As a yogic counterpose to the world outside, I'll make it with my peace of mind and love of imperfection.

Once I've set it going, it will look after itself and show little sign of my having been here. There will be a few small jobs from time to time, a little weeding or cutting back when some of the more aggressive plants try to take advantage of more delicate things, to keep it all in balance, but nothing arduous or irritating. The leaves will be brushed off the path and will lie on the earth where they belong; the seed heads will be left to stand, they'll frost in winter and feed the blue tits, and turn to dust and clump and spread to make their own little habitats, and it will feel as natural as if it had been ignored and forgotten while we changed the world around it, and will be as it was meant to be.

11

RAIN

Ant hills, molehills, pigtails, poison

I am small and he is strong
One day he will be old and weak
And I will still be young and strong.

Oh, magpies with your crarking tongue
Who like to pick up shiny things
Come down and take his eyes.

Ants leave little hills of fine sandy soil on the cracks between the paving stones where they come up near the house. The Angry Dog pours a kettle of boiling water over them. The boy tells him that he loves them, that they are harmless, but Dog tells him not to be so stupid, ants bite and will invade the house and live in the sugar bowl, and the boy is frustrated by trying to explain things to people who think that because they have power, they know everything there is to know. Power is rarely intelligent; more commonly it is selfish and insensitive, gained and maintained through oppression or exploitation. There's another kind of quiet power, rarer and more dignified, that is usually unnoticed, hidden in the brutal noise; it's quiet and filled with peace and the boy can feel it, knows that it is real, he feels it in his body but does not yet know what it is.

Typewriter-rain falls in the small puddles, tapping like an infinite number of monkeys at a keyboard, writing gibberish. It falls straight down from a sky that looks drawn and shaded with a soft pencil, and makes shallow lakes that reflect the bare branches and white sky above them. Under the old damson tree at the bottom of the garden there has, over the past couple of weeks, appeared a row of little mounds of dark and crumbly soil. As the boy runs down to his shed through the rain after school he's thinking, 'That idiot Dog won't know what Aconite is—I could put it in his bowl and he would eat it!' As he playfully imagines his father with his eyes popping out and grasping at his throat with both hands, and writhing to the ground burbling, he is distracted by a fresh mound of soil that's moving, growing from below, but that stops moving as soon as he sees it. He gets a bit closer and sits on his haunches to watch what happens. He remains squatting in stillness.

For any young boy, time is a liquid that speeds up in the narrows and slows down when it's wide or deep, and sometimes even stops to whirl around in eddies. Depending on how interesting, how wide or deep, something could be stuck circling in the same place for seconds or days. He is there long enough for his shirt to get soaked while his mother watches her idiot son from the kitchen window and wonders what he is up to. The rain gives him silver pigtails of water that hang down into the collar of his school shirt, which sticks to his back, becomes transparent, shows his white skin and pointy shoulder blades.

He squats and looks at the little pile of earth. What was pushing the soil up? It went still when it heard him coming, like he does when he hears the Angry Dog. Is it a gas pipe leaking, about to explode, or an underground stream or a root? But he knows it must be an animal, and the only

85

creature he can think of is a rat. He wants to get his trowel and dig to have a look, but a rat might be waiting to leap, to run up his body with its massive filthy claws and drive its yellow fangs into him and eat its way though his body to escape, like a boy at school told him would happen if he cornered one. So he decides to give it a wide berth. He squats and looks, but nothing happens, then he goes and kicks the little hill, runs and watches from his shed doorway, thinking that if a rat comes out, he can slam the door until it goes away.

As he gets to his shed a mottled cat pushes out through the gap in the warped wooden door and walks off quickly through the rain, without looking back. She turns under the bushes, sits on her haunches and elegantly stretches a back leg and licks it, pushing her tongue right down between the toes. This brown-and-orange cat is often in the bushes at the bottom of the garden; if he goes towards her, she gets up and wanders off, always slow and elegant; she never runs, but is always somehow much faster than he is. If he leaves her alone, she sits and sometimes curls to sleep. She doesn't mind him being there, but doesn't want his attention.

The peas are taller and bushier as they climb, with twining monkey-fingers, spiralling through twigs stuck in the earth. A few green shoots have appeared in the plot and he wonders if it's the radishes at first, but they are scattered around and not in the rows he planted, so they must be weeds. The buds on the damson tree are ready to crack, on the edge of exposing their inner parts. It feels like the world is waking up and reaching out. Because of his wet shirt he feels cold, so he runs back inside the house, goes to his room, puts his shirt on a hanger to dry, then digs out a T-shirt, a jumper, his coat and goes back out to the shed, where his books are lined up on the bench ready for inspection.

12

GARDENER

A length of string, a blue wheelbarrow

A NEW SHED AND PATH

I've tied a piece of string between two sticks and stuck them in the ground, so the line is tight and straight between them, where the edge of the path will be. The plants, when they come, will fall over the path and soften its sharpness. It needs to be straight because this space is small and it will be underneath the washing line. I am kneeling next to the apple tree, pouring bags of sand for the base of the brick path. It feels good to have dirt under my nails again. I tamp down the sand to make it level and firm it with a lump hammer and plank, then lay the bricks on top to touch the string line to the left, tap them into place, tap-tap, with the shock-absorbing handle of the hammer, which is hickory, like my walking stick. It's a fluid rhythm, but hard work, and I manage to lay about two feet each day, crawling slug-like past the apple tree and the sage plants and under the lilac by the ferns.

Down here and moving slowly, the garden seems much larger. I stop the tap-tapping now and then to sit on the step and have a cup of tea, or watch the birds or leaves in the breeze, to rest my knees. When I lift a brick off the pile that's been squatting there for a while, a nest of centipedes scatters off. Woodlice and slugs have already found refuge there and the robin waits nearby for his chance. There is so much peace in physical work—one simple task naturally follows another. I lay the bricks in a basketweave pattern, two pointing this way, then two that, crawling slowly along as the path trails out behind me. It is simple repetitive work, like much of gardening, and it takes a toll on the knees, and so I take a day off here and there to walk and stretch my muscles and rest. Two weeks later I get to the end, to the base of the fence where it's shady, and there I tap a pink rhododendron from its pot, dig and fill a hole with water. I have always done it that way round: water the pot, dig the hole, fill the hole with water, put the plant in the hole and backfill the soil.

Structural things can happen fast, depending on how quickly you work and can get materials, but most things happen at the seasonal speed of nature. I myself happen more at that speed these days, and I wonder if I've taken too much on. I need to use my stick more often, and twice this week I've fallen asleep in the chair while I was reading. I decide to have a few days off. The path is far from finished, but of course that familiar tension arises and builds until the need to get on with it is more powerful than my resistance. On the third day I use my blue wheelbarrow to take five tons of gravel, which have been tipped onto the drive, through the house and up the new path, and pour it to the left to make a new base for the shed. And while I push, I add to the canon of wheelbarrow poems with a haiku of my own:

A blue wheelbarrow
empty now then full again
squeaking in complaint.

When the job is done, I am exhausted and go on the internet for three days to choose a new shed. I know exactly what I want my shed to look like and how big it will be, but finding it is not so easy and it is a while before I spot the right thing: small with a square window that will look up at the house. I hesitate, because a shed is not cheap and my bank account is threadbare, but I've invested so much already that I cannot stop. I fill in the online form and I get an email telling me it will arrive in about a week. No humans were involved in the transaction, no eye met eye, no flesh touched flesh, no voices heard or words exchanged, no cash changed hands and funds just flew, as they do, away.

WE MEET IN the evening, and Peggy and I make tea together. We sit at the round kitchen table with the back door open and talk about our day, and listen while the wood pigeons sit on the fence and watch us with their lovely stupid faces; we eat noodles and tofu in a green Thai sauce that she makes herself in the bullet machine. I'm vegetarian, so she eats a lot of vegetarian food too. Food and love. Everything else is a support structure for that: gardening is love, writing is love and we both love our life together and our individual lives that we share. It is all so very simple.

She grew up on a mountain in Wales in a solitary old house full of books, and a lighthouse illuminated her nights, its foghorn on her foggy days. Waking and sleep intermingle for both of us. We both know solitude and love it. We laugh. We understand the accidental damage people do, and we forgive. She is not perfect, I am not perfect—not perfect is perfect for us. She writes mysterious stories about relationships, children, love, which she makes up in her head. I build gardens in words and in images and in the earth. We support each other's work. We are both tender creatures and a stifled creative impulse is a little piece of death, so we take care. We are flowers that lean together. Over dinner Peggy tells me about one of her characters that might have to go, because she doesn't lead her story anywhere. I offer another point of view when she asks for one, and she does the same for me.

Early in my gardening career I wore a green polo-neck shirt and hat with my name and phone number embroidered on it in sunny yellow, and I had one made for her too, and she would come out with me some days and drive the big petrol mower, making stripes, or do some weeding next to me. We would pretend she was 'Bob', my apprentice. Now she writes stories at the top of our house, watching seagulls pass, and I write poetry at the bottom, near the garden. I read it to her, we drink tea and wait for the cherry tree to blossom. Sometimes we visit our son and his family in France, our daughter in town, we go to the opera or the cinema, the local Indian restaurant or the pub. We both love classy footwear and clothes made of natural fabrics, fresh vegetables, good cheese, wandering around places we haven't been to before, and we chatter unceasingly. I sit on banquettes for hours in clothes shops while she tries things on. We hold hands when we walk, we hold hands in bed, I polish her shoes and sing to her. We do our separate work in solitude—our creativity spouts from silence—but at the end of each day we come back together and clatter and steam and eat. Our heads still full of the chattering characters we're writing about, till they fade and go to sleep, and then we talk. Our work and life together are what our life is all about. The garden, the writing, the cooking and eating, the outings. We know each other's weak points; she knows my tender spots and nurses them, protects them, as I do hers. Sometimes we get it wrong and irritate a sensitivity and argue or get upset, then we forgive. We have intense internal lives and because we do not need each other, we love each other freely, without fear.

Tin-can radio, Slow the slug

The boy is in his shed with two empty baked-bean tins, a nail and some garden string. He had washed the cans and peeled off the labels so they're clean. He bangs a hole in the centre of their round bases with a nail and his hammer, threads the fiddly string through from the outside into the can and ties a knot to hold it secure, and again with the other end of the string to the other can, then runs inside with one of the cans and hands it to his mum.

'Hold the string tight, Mum, and listen—see if it works.' He strolls purposefully back down the garden, head held high and businesslike, and speaks into the tin-can radio. His mum isn't holding it tight. She is busy wiping the table. 'Hold it tight, Mum, listen!' he yells, and she briefly holds the can to her ear, but as he pulls the string tight, it moves away from her. 'HOLD IT TIGHT TO YOUR EAR!' he shouts, clearly and slowly, from the other end of the garden, so she pulls it tight and he starts to talk, and the string goes tighter still as she walks and dusts at the same time and the string bends around the door frame. 'MUM! It won't work if the string touches anything!' he shouts.

'I'm sorry, love, I'm busy,' she says and means it, kindly, but she really doesn't understand what he wants of her. He feels like he's talking to a ghost who wanders in and out, broadcast like the shadows on the TV screen, disconnected from this earthly realm. He has shouted at her twice now, and shouting attracts unwanted attention, so 'Never mind,' he says, and 'Sorry, love,' she says. 'I've got a lot to do, maybe later, eh? Why don't you ask one of your brothers?'

And he wonders if he might, but knows that neither of them, who prefer to play with a ball in the street or run around pretending to shoot each other and die, will take his experiment seriously and will just mess about or try to take control. So he winds the string around the silent can and takes it back to his shed. He likes to run with his brothers sometimes and pretend to die, but it gets a bit dull if it goes on all day and, to be honest, they can be a bit bossy if it doesn't go their way, so he tends to leave them to their games and get on with his work.

ON THE PATH a silver trail and, at its end, a brown slug two whole inches long. A bubble of mucus on the hole in its side inflates and pops, and he prods the hole with a blade of grass and then again and, at the third prod, the slug contracts into a small hard lump and bubbles out slime from underneath. The boy picks it up; it's sucking itself to the ground, hanging on tight like a limpet, so he has to dig his fingers hard under its frilly orange edge and peel it from the ground, and it rolls a little tighter in his fingers like a knot of muscle. Cold and damp and slimy, hard like an unripe plum, juicy and moist and biteable on his palm. He carries it in his hand; and slowly the slug uncurls, extends itself a little, its antlers reach out and wave: the big ones with eyes on the ends look at him as he looks back; the little ones point down like feelers and, below them, the slit of a mouth. After a while the slug rasps at his hand as it has a taste of the dirt and the skin of his palm. Its mouth is strong and the boy can feel his skin being grated away, so he puts the slug down on the grass, runs inside and finds a pickle jar in the kitchen bin, washes it out, and when he gets back to the path the slug has moved about two feet into the damp lawn.

'You are slow, aren't you, little fella?' he says and picks the slug up. 'Come on, Slow,' he says and pops it in the jar. He tries to wipe the slime off his fingers onto the grass, but it won't budge and he scrapes it hard and it still won't shift, and he thinks, 'If I ever need some glue, I'll find a slug' and pointlessly wipes his hands on his trousers, spreading the mess, but not making anything any less sticky. He puts a few blades of grass and some torn-off bits of dandelion leaves in the jar, puts the lid on his workbench and, with the nail and the hammer, punches two jagged holes so that the slug can breathe.

'Slow' goes to live in the jar on the bench. The boy looks up 'slug' in his books and learns that the breathing hole in the slug's side is the entrance to his/her single lung and that under the cloak on his back, the mantle, there is the remainder of a shell, the remnants of the snail that the slug evolved from. He reads of his massive corkscrew penis that's half the length of his body and, like the angels, he is both male and female; he eats greenery or worms, or lichen, depending on what kind of slug he is, but from the ancient, damp engravings the boy can't work out his breed. He watches it breathe through its blowhole like a whale, and the waves that ripple along its foot as it climbs around the glass.

After a few days, Slow is looking ropey, lethargic; he hasn't touched his grass or leaves and has left strings of black shit around the jar. In fact he smells a bit. Over the next few days the smell gets worse, and the boy feels guilty that what he wanted was more important to him than what the slug needed, that maybe Slow is dying and doesn't want to be a prisoner. Like Antaeus, he has lost his contact with the earth and his strength is fading. He needs to be free, to be whoever he is. The boy tries different food, but nothing helps, and after a week he lies on the ground and shakes the lethargic slug onto the lawn under the tree and waits for him to unroll. Slow is released back to the wild, thinner, drier and slower. There are ants down in the grass and a black beetle wanders by, its skinny legs testing and struggling across the rough earth while the boy lies there and watches Slow slowly unroll and wander off to continue his own life, in his own way.

GARDENER

A walk down by the eye-spikes, a dog, a ghost, a green man

❋ ❀ ❋ ❀

I need to pause for a while. A garden should evolve, it's a continuing conversation, like a painting, rather than engineering a machine to the precision of a plan. Living things are wobbly, and one thing in the garden changes everything around. We are not working merely with inert stems and leaves and flowers; each thing you plant casts a shadow, makes a dry patch at its base and dampness in a circle, round which the rain drips off its leaves. More complicated than that is the visual dynamic between a leafy thing, a stemmy thing, a spiky thing and things that are tall and thin or low and flat, and the fact that in a few months' time they will all look completely different.

I wait for the shed, take a few days off, let my body sleep when it wants and wake when it wants, and my days align

to the dawn and dusk. Just after the blackbird and the robins, the sparrows begin to sing and chirp, the sun rises red
through the street trees in front of the house and the sky
goes pink for a while, then I hear the crows chatter and I
sit on my mat for an hour. The days begin like this. They
end when the sun drops down over the roof of the house
behind, and I go inside and we cook and talk and laugh
and eat, and I light the fire and sit in my junk-shop chair
and read.

I put on my jacket to go and buy flowers for the kitchen
table, and to stretch my legs. As I amble around the village
where I was a gardener for so many years I see the flowers I planted in the little front gardens of people who've
since died, moved house or just grown old, and I feel that
I have added love. Most people won't consciously notice
them, but will still have their day lifted. I planted when it
was time to plant, pruned when it was time to prune and
mowed when it was time to mow, and these things added
to the sum total of beauty and politeness and positivity of
the daily world. The roses reach up with new red stems like
children's feeble grasping hands, trees are budding, tulips
peek their red beaks from the soil and open daffodils are
sucking at the sun. As I walk through the streets I think, 'I
planted that, I planted that, I planted that', at apple trees
and magnolias and roses and spring bulbs, and feel I've
done a good thing.

More than the things I planted, I love the things that
got there on their own, the wild anarchic things: the scarlet
pimpernel, forget-me-nots and shepherd's purse that grow

99

in the dust in the pavements at the base of people's walls, where the ants come out, leaving sand. I love the mosses in the gutters at the edge of the road, and the lichens that grow on stone footpaths, and the dandelions in the cracks between them that are walked on every day by clergy and congregation and shoppers and schoolchildren and old people from the homes with their sticks and wheelchairs, and yet they thrive together, all together. I love these plants so much; they hang on tight and wild, and I think of them as punks like me who say, 'Up yours! I'm doing my thing exactly where and when I please!' And they need nothing, they need no one—only the bees that visit from time to time, as they glow in the sun against the warm golden stone, which holds crystals of mica that sparkle in the sun.

The air feels so clean that I take a detour to see if I can collect some seed heads from the dog walkers' field near the church that snuggles in the dip it was built in, to hide it from raiding Vikings. A dead stone-winged soldier looks down on me from a tower, a warrior angel with a sword. A rusted iron railing, waist-high, leans and twists like a sinuous dragon, frozen and growing through a tree here and there. I notice that the rust-sharpened spikes on its back are two pupils'-width apart; the thought gives me the shudders, and I keep my distance as it snakes past the graves of clerics in their special, holier part of the field. Over the little stone humpback bridge that leaps a dried-up waterway choked with trees, then the fields of those who 'rest' and 'sleep' under stones washed in river mist. Massed blue stars of forget-me-nots strain at their green leads, as if eager to escape and release their yellow suns to the sky. Massive ancient yews, whose roots burst like yet more dragons coiling from the stone walls built of boulders to contain them.

I swing my stick past the quietly tilted lichened stones that mark the composting dead, where robins and thrushes and blackbirds sit, then flit into brambles as I approach. From between the graves there's barking; a dog runs out towards me, stops, leans back and bares its teeth and barks. Its owner comes from behind one of the dragon yews and trots up, calling, 'Snowy!' or 'Chloe!' or something I can't make out above the noise. But it won't return to her, and it leans back and bares its teeth and stamps as it barks and readies itself to attack. For some reason it is afraid— perhaps it came upon me unexpectedly—and fear, like selfishness and greed, as we are all too aware, often ends in violence.

In a flash, my every muscle tensed, I drop into a quiet mental zone and whisper, 'Shhh' as time expands and stretches out, to unroll a dozen scenarios in my head. I don't have time to feel afraid. I stand tree-still and wait for the dog's attack. There is no point running; it would be faster than me, and I wouldn't be able to protect myself if my back were towards its teeth. I consider whether I should wait until it leaps, then whack it as hard as I can on the head with my heavy walking stick, which automatically I am holding ready, or maybe tempting it to bite the stick instead of me while I . . . do what? I decide that when the dog's back legs spring, all I can do is my very best to send it whelping into the trees. As I prepare for the battle of my life, the owner clips it to its lead and repeats over and over, 'I'm so sorry, I'm so sorry' and 'He wouldn't harm a fly.'

As they leave, the adrenaline comes and, with it, a bit of a crisis. My heart has an intermittent electrical problem; every morning and evening I take a bunch of pills to keep it in rhythm, and stop my blood from clotting in a ventricle and killing me or giving me a stroke, should it become chaotic. Adrenaline has naturally increased my heart rate, as it's supposed to do, but the overloaded circuits have tripped and my heart is not beating, but quivering more than 250 times per minute—it has lost its rhythm and become chaotic. Leaning on my stick, I walk to a bench, hook the stick on its back and sit to observe the pain in my chest. My heart is banging so hard I can feel its throb in my skin, my neck, my temples, my thighs and my arms and ears, even in my eyes. I am alone here. The main road is fifteen minutes away, up a very steep hill. I relax my muscles, lower my eyes, lift my head and balance it on my neck, ears over shoulders and shoulders over hips, in my meditation posture. I'm a tree, a rock, a river. I put my hands in my lap, left over right, to make a bowl. I am not afraid, so there's no clinging. I let go of feelings, of the desire for things to be different, quieten my mind and watch the breath. There is pain, but it is just pain. There is throbbing, but it is just throbbing. Breath goes in, breath goes out, until there's only universal breath moving one way, then another. I am silent, inside and out, apart from nature's distant beat somewhere in the world; the birds sing, the breeze moves, the leaves rustle.

I let go of the little mind and find the bigger one and slow my heart rate down. I'm good at this, but can't do anything about the rhythm; it settles in its own time, sometimes overnight. I am familiar with my heart and its ways.

From the corner of my eye I see a man dressed in black and I know, beyond any doubt, that he isn't really there. Even though nearly everyone here is dead and their dreams are over, we who live, still dream. I turn to see him properly and he is gone. I'm not sure if I saw a ghost or, being closer to my own death, only imagined it, or did he merely wander off into the trees, perhaps a homeless man.

Peggy says that I'm susceptible to ghosts. Every now and then I'll see a shadow go by and look up, and she will ask what I'm looking at, then tell me nothing passed; a few times I have seen people who Peggy swears were not there, when I mention their hat or dark clothing. I say she simply didn't notice them. I have no explanation for them. I don't have an explanation for the forsythia growing next to me, either, even though that is as real as anything ever is. Life expresses itself as a thing that expands into form, then contracts into chaos. I get up from my bench and wander over to where I glimpsed him and stand beside a new grave—the flowers are wilted, but still have colour in them. There is no marker yet. My heart is still irregular, missing beats, adding beats, but is slowing down.

I leave the bone-yard and walk through trees that, despite their age and brokenness, still grow and flower and seed. Natural pools between old roots, where birds and insects drink, where foxgloves gape and ferns unfurl. Past the dog walkers' field of grasses and sedges and buttercups and cow parsley and nettles and clover, edged by tiny celandine and a handful of hiding orchids, and down to the sunlit rocks by the river's edge, where water trickles and flashes. A grey heron, almost indistinguishable from the grasses on the banks, stands with his spear poised, pointed between the rocks that narrow the flow and make the water fast and white.

I return past the eye-spikes and over the bridge of the dead, cutting through the greyness on my own with not another soul about until, at the road crossing, as I wait for the man to turn green, I swap a smile and a 'good morning' with an old lady in a fleece and joggers, who came from the other way. The green man flashes and peeps and the old lady and I cross, we turn our separate ways and leave each other behind. For a moment the isolation is broken and, in that break, an awareness that those little connections are important, and I want more. I've never been good at them. I am unsocialised. I always tried to do what other people told me was right: to be a normal person in a social world, to chat about the neighbours and politics and right and wrong, to complain about the seagulls or the bin men or the internet. I tried to be spontaneous, but heard myself say stupid things, or things that were untrue, just for something to say, trying to fit in. I am called 'the cat that walks alone' or 'he walks to the beat of his own drummer' or 'a square peg in a round hole'. The truth is that I couldn't see any value in talking or even thinking about these things. I found my true self when I saw that the 'self' is merely an illusion—there is no such thing as a separate 'self', only the stream. This idea of self makes Ego; it separates us from the animals and so destroys our world. It is not good to feel separate from the animals.

My swing has gone, my body tired, my heart heavy and uneven, and it gives me a hollow feeling that feels like hunger. I want to eat—I want to eat everything that exists. I turn the corner into my street; there's a lorry outside my house and a man is lowering my new shed down to the path with a crane; before I get there he drives off and I consider waving a thanks to him, but he has no idea who I am, just some random old geezer waving at strangers.

Home, I take off my tired old brown corduroy jacket that I have worn since I was a molecatcher; it is an affectation, and I wear it because I think it makes me look like Mr Mole. I have matching brown corduroy trousers with braces and a gold badge of a mole on the collar. I make a pot of tea and lower myself into my chair, put my blanket across my knees and remember that I went out to buy flowers. My heart is slow, irregular with the odd extra and missing beat, but later in the evening as we chat it's back to normal again. I tell Peggy and she smiles and says, 'Good.' She knows when it's happening; she says that I get black rings around my eyes and sometimes she hears me gasp for air, although I try to do it quietly, my mouth wide open and turned away, so she doesn't notice.

Rhubarb leaves and monkshood, Grandma's cows and dowsing

A MOLE!

Nobody in the family eats the rhubarb that grows in massive ancient clumps on the other side of the garden. His mother tells him that when she was a child she used to eat the stems dipped in sugar, and she gives him a little bowl of sugar to take down the garden. 'But don't eat the leaves,' she says, 'they are poisonous.' He slices off the leaves and, sitting on the step, he dips an acid-pink stem in the sugar and nibbles on it; the taste is juicy and astringent and tainted with the three-in-one oil that he has lubricated his penknife hinge with. The cross-section of rhubarb reminds him of the layers of the tree trunk he found in the encyclopaedia, except that it isn't put together the same way at all. It is shaped like the capital letter D, red on the outside, but a beautiful pale green inside and full of white dots. His books tell him nothing about it, but do say that the leaves contain oxalic acid, and that people have died after cooking and eating them like spinach, which gives him an idea.

'Rhubarb leaves and monkshood.' He writes next to the drawing he makes of the monkshood flower, colours it in with crayons and then a cross-section of rhubarb stem and a leaf. His summer is spent drawing leaves and trees and flowers, details, making notes, trying to draw a rose flower, again and again, until he becomes so frustrated that he's angry. He tries to draw the raindrops that settle like glass beads into the centre of nasturtium leaves. He struggles to make the reflections look lifelike, but is getting good at drawing stylised clouds and rain, splashes, little details that are not complete pictures, but fragments, ideas copied from the encyclopaedia, where he sees engravings with skies by William Blake.

At school his art teacher asks him why he never finishes anything—he doesn't know, he says. He doesn't need to, isn't interested in finishing. His drawings are tools; they are not made to decorate the walls or look pretty, they are made to explore and understand. They often have words next to them: 'The drops of water on the leaves always roll down to the middle,' he writes, after testing his observation by tilting the nasturtium leaves and watching the silvery bobble roll, and seeing reflected in its almost perfect mercury sphere the house behind, the damson tree in front, highlights and shadows, a blue sky and clouds in a crystal ball that holds and shows him all the world around. Deeper, closer still, he sees his own distorted eye filling the globe, the boy, his eye, the house, the tree, the leaf, the raindrop all together, all one thing and equal against the sky. It is perfect and he's filled with love for it. He lets go of the leaf, and the silver raindrop rolls back to the middle.

The back door opens and Angry Dog trots out excitedly with a man he's never seen before, they talk and point down the garden to where the boy is. The man is dressed in old brown clothes and a flat cap and is dusty with soil; he has a ponytail and a beard and carries a stick and a big dirty bag over his shoulder. He walks down alone, says, 'Mornin'' to the boy, seems friendly and nice, and the boy—whose mind is in overdrive, wondering if he's come to see him, and then, 'Maybe he's my real father' (as all children wonder from time to time)—asks, 'Who are you?' After he's said it, he thinks that might have sounded rude, and he doesn't like to be rude, thinks it is rude to be rude. He looks back up to the house to see the Angry Dog leaning in the doorway, smoking and looking down to where they are.

The man smiles and says, 'I'm here to deal with your little visitor', nodding to the small mounds of soil, which have increased in number every day since the boy first noticed them. He wanders around for a while, then starts prodding in the ground with his pointed stick. Eventually he kneels down, takes a trowel out of his bag and digs a little hole, puts a metal contraption of levers and springs in the hole and covers it with turf, then he pushes a stick in the ground with a white painted end to mark where it is buried.

The boy has retired to the step of his shed to watch, and Angry Dog has gone indoors; the boy sits watching, chin in hands, elbows on knees, as the man wanders up and down the garden, prodding and kneeling and digging and burying his springs and levers in the soil. He does this three times, getting closer to the boy, who asks, 'What are you doing?'

The man tells him that he is looking for mole tunnels and putting traps in them.

'What's a mole like?' the boy asks.

'It's a little animal with great big hands,' the moleman says, 'that will dig tunnels all over your garden until there are piles of soil everywhere.'

'What's your name? Why do you want to catch it?'

'Because it's my job. Some people don't want their grass ruined,' he says. 'I don't mind them, I like them, but it's my job.'

'Do you catch lots of moles?'

'Yes,' the moleman says, 'hundreds and hundreds.'

'What do you do with them? Are they dangerous?'

'No, but they can do a lot of damage.'

'Are there hundreds down there?'

'Probably only one, maybe two . . . Now see these sticks that I have put in the ground, you mustn't go anywhere near them, because there are traps there and they could chop your fingers right off, okay?'

'Okay, I'll stay away,' says the boy, and he follows the moleman to the house, asking questions. 'How did it get there? What do you do with them? What do they look like? Can I keep it as a pet? How do you find them under the ground?'

'It's like dowsing,' he says.

'What's dowsing?'

'Like a feeling in my bones—I just know where they are.' The man briefly answers that they don't make very good pets and knocks on the door.

The Angry Dog seems calm today and takes him inside, and the boy goes to have a closer look at the traps. He imagines pandemonium in an underground world, a universe of animals in lairs, and hollows and tunnels through caves with rocks and roots hanging down, beetles and worms in a world that can never be seen. All that's on the surface are the white painted sticks and little mounds of soil, one of which he prods with a twig until he hears a 'snap' and a spring of metal wire pops out of the ground. He has done something wrong again and, as usual, he decides to say nothing about it and pretend it wasn't him. 'It must have been a bird or something,' he thinks, 'if anybody asks.'

He looks in his books for dowsing, but it isn't there, so he asks the Angry Dog, 'What's dowsing, Dad?'

'It's nonsense, Son,' he says.

The Angry Dog isn't much of a gardener. He cuts the grass when it's sunny and when he can be bothered, but he doesn't care about it; it belongs to the landlord and the boy supposes that the landlord has sent the moleman.

Each day the boy comes home from school and looks to see if there are any more molehills, but from that day on there are no more. And after a week the sticks are gone, the traps gone, the moleman has been back and taken them away—he has dowsed the moles straight out of the ground. In his books the boy reads about moles and copies a picture of one, but it's hard to tell what it's of, because there is not much to a mole.

HIS GRANDMOTHER ARRIVES. She is a big woolly woman who lets out a large sigh as she lowers herself down to the armchair, then drops the last two inches with a thump and a squeak of the springs. Leaning into her massive woolly bag, she pulls out a jumper that she holds up to him, which is too small and 'will do for one of the others', plus a bag of day-old cakes from the bakery she works at, balls of wool and needles, and then sits knitting and smoking at the same time, with her cigarette in the corner of her mouth; with the ash growing longer and longer, she chats with his mum about people he has never heard of. She seems to be knitting another jumper that won't fit.

'What's dowsing, Nana?' he asks her when they go quiet. 'The moleman said he was dowsing.'

'Oh, we had a dowser come to the farm to find water for the cows,' she says. It is the first the boy has heard about a farm. After the inevitable barrage of questions, he learns that in the war his grandmother worked on a farm for a while, looking after milk-cows. 'I sat on a stool and milked one hundred and fifty cows by hand,' she tells him, 'one cow after another, and then in the evening I would have to do it all again.'

'Did the cows like being milked?'

'They loved it!' she says and laughs. 'Some of the girls were cruel and came from the town and didn't understand the cows, but I took to them straight away and they took to me. I'd love to have a cow!'

'I'd like to have a cow too.'

And they laugh at the idea of a cow living in the little garden. His nana says that you have to be kind, because cows are warm and friendly and intelligent, and they would kick the girls who were too rough and snuggled up to the kind ones.

She says, 'A dowser can find water and other things that are under the ground, or even things that are lost, by using a twig or a pendulum or metal rods. I can dowse,' she goes on. 'I can find lost keys. I've done it. I found a wedding ring once and,' she says slowly, looking directly at him, which lets him know that this is particularly special, 'I can tell whether a pregnant woman or animal is going to have a boy or a girl. I tie a wedding ring on a piece of cotton and hold it over the woman's stomach; if it swings in a straight line, she will have a boy, and in a circle means she will have a girl. I have done it a hundred times and I am always right. Always right,' she says again, while looking him straight in the eye because she wants him to know it is true, despite the Angry Dog's grumbling in the corner.

She pulls her thin wedding ring across the papery skin of her yellow finger, and he watches her loose skin as it folds over, then under the ring, and pulls tight as she works it down.

'Here,' she says, handing it to him, 'tie this piece of wool to it.' And he ties the piece of bright-green wool she gives him to the ring. 'That's right,' she says. 'Now ask it a question—it is always right, you'll see.' And they ask it questions. 'A circle means yes,' she says, 'and a straight line means no.'

'Will I be a great artist?' he asks. 'No.'

'Will I be a policeman? No.'

'A soldier? No.'

'Will I get married? Yes.'

'Will I have children? Yes.'

'Will I be rich? No.'

'Will I be poor? Yes', then 'No', then 'Yes' again. By this time he is wondering if his nana is making the ring say what she wants it to say.

'Will there be chips for tea? No.'

And all these things came true.

Later he goes out to his shed and brings in one of the encyclopaedia volumes. He wants to impress her with something of his own, to show her, to make her proud of him studying and learning with his heavy, serious book, and he knows that she will not make fun of him. He curls at her feet while she knits and he flicks through the pages.

'You are a little professor, aren't you?' Nana says.

'He's too stupid to come in out of the rain,' says Angry Dog, who is adding to the fug of smoke and trying to fix a broken tin opener with his pliers. 'Why are you showing him that old witchy nonsense anyway?'

'He's an old soul,' she replies, 'he should be left to find his way. Your father doesn't understand,' she continues in a quiet voice, 'but we know, don't we?'

He nods, smiling, but doesn't really know what it is that they are both supposed to know.

He hasn't felt human warmth for a long time. Hasn't touched a hand, a face, been held—no physical contact, other than feeling the odd slap. He puts his hand on hers, on her thin skin, and it feels a bit wrong to be touching her, but she smiles at him sadly, puts her other hand on top of his and whispers, 'It is going to be okay, you know' and she has tears in her eyes.

'Is it better when you are older?' he asks quietly, trying hard to say it without attracting the Angry Dog's attention.

She smiles and, after a pause to think, 'It's different,' she says.

Angry Dog snorts.

The boy swings the pendulum, asking only with his mind and eyes, 'Is it going to be okay?'

'Yes,' the pendulum says.

'Will he kill me? No.'

He stops short of asking if he will kill the Angry Dog. He doesn't want that particular act to be set in stone.

Today Angry Dog has given him rain, and his grandmother has given him sun, and he is learning to be a separate independent thing. Rain will make him strong and sun will let him blossom, and all he has to do is endure.

GARDENER

I need three hands, a list of plants, sorting seeds, sparkling water

I level the gravel base by dragging the edge of a plank backwards and forwards across it, stamping the gravel down, testing it with a spirit level and then repeating the dragging and stamping until it's level and flat. The shed is on the pavement at the front of the house. I cut away the straps and polythene sheeting that the flat-packed shed is wrapped in. Four walls, one floor, two roof sections, a door, a few extra bits of wood for edging, a roll of roofing felt and a pane of glass for the window.

I carry the pieces through the house and put them together. It's a bit of a balancing act at the beginning, but leaning two adjacent walls against each other, holding them with one hand, kicking them into alignment with my foot and using an electric screwdriver with the other hand, I can make a corner that stands on its own. From then on it's easy; the walls go up, the roof goes on, the door is fitted. Erecting the shed takes two hours. I go inside it, close the door, come out again, close the door, open the door and go back in. Like a cat, in and out for a while, testing it, smelling it, understanding this new space. I bring out a stool and sit in the shed and look through the window at the house. All that's left to do is paint it. At some point I will paint it. I expect I will paint it.

What was once just a space has become a place again. Outside the shed door is the lilac tree. At its base in the shade I have put a wooden half-barrel to create a hollow where water gathers and ferns and hart's-tongues can dip in. Magpies find it within a couple of days and stand at the edge to drink, then robins and sparrows and blue tits. Behind the old shed there was a log pile; a few large trunks were rotting at the bottom, pine and beech that I hadn't got round to cutting into stove lengths, and I stack them up as a stumpery by the fence, for beetles and slugs and snails and fungus. White mycelium is spreading through them and the smell is delicious and fruity; herds of wood-lice fall off as I move them and wander confused by my feet, tickle my grubby hands and try to cling to the logs that are hollowed out in places, with slugs nestled in cracks. I plant a rhododendron behind the untidy pile of logs and more ferns in front, then there's bare soil where the leaves will fall and woodland flowers will come in the autumn and spring: cyclamens and colchicums and bluebells, wild garlic.

Making a garden is like making a drawing or writing a story: you know the outline and where it begins and ends, but the details sometimes change, a happy accident is incorporated and the foggy plan alters. Putting things in, rubbing things out, redrawing and blurring, and slowly it starts to look nearly but not quite right and then one little smudge of shadow and it all clicks into place.

The path goes up the middle, between the lilac and apple trees on the right and the shed on the left. In the bare patch where the workshop stood I'll put some taller plants behind the hydrangea—angelica perhaps. There is ivy on the fence and, overhanging from the other side, a holly where the sparrows sing, and a firethorn. The garden is mostly shady, so I need to choose appropriate plants for shade, but also to make it as wild as possible. I'll keep the established shrubs but blend them in with new plantings. The hydrangeas don't feel very wild until their flowers fade and turn to rust and gold, like an autumn woodland.

List of plants for a shady woodland garden
FOXGLOVES, at the edges where it's dappled and the soil drains well
ANGELICA, tall and statuesque, will give seeds to the birds in winter
DILL, an umbellifer with ferny leaves and seeds that I can use in the kitchen
FERNS, shuttlecocks and hart's-tongues
SNOWDROPS everywhere
WOOD ANEMONES at the edge of the woodland path
CYCLAMEN COUM to flower in the winter
BLUEBELLS, of course, the native ones
PYRACANTHAS for by the back fence: red berries in winter for the birds and blackbirds like to nest there
PRIMROSES
CAMPION
SWEET WOODRUFF
NARCISSUS to come before the spring blossom and planted between everything
WILD GARLIC for the pot, which will spread and flower before the lilac leaves come and the sky shades over.

Once this is done, it will be a truly 'low-maintenance garden' and over the years, as the woodland flowers naturalise and spread, all I'll have to do from time to time is weed a little, move a fallen branch to somewhere it looks good.

I'm sorting packets of seeds on the kitchen table. Playing like a serious child. These seeds make me deeply happy. I recognise the tiny blue-black poppy seeds, the smaller dusty foxgloves and the long black cosmos and crinkly crescent marigold seeds as easily as I recognise my own family, and in my hand they feel magical because I know their power, know their stories past and future, but I will never comprehend exactly how and why they work. There are only two kinds of knowledge we can have about a thing: we can say what the thing is made of and we can say what the thing does. Anything else is mystery and up for debate.

I often had seeds in my pockets when I was a gardener. I put a handful in my trouser pocket, just to feel them there— they are my kin. These will be the last seeds I sow, because if they grow they will seed themselves and I won't make another garden after this.

I feel at home with them, and that boy felt—feels—felt the same. I know they excited him as much as they do me. For the briefest moment of time I wonder who did it first, who walked around with seeds in his trouser pockets: was it me or him who first had a pocket of magic beans? Does time go this way *and* that? I know that's nonsense, but somehow the connection between us felt tight for a second, as if he were on the other end of a tin-can telephone and the string between us was tight, the signal clear and strong. Between us is the unstable thread of time. But so much has happened in that time—friends and lovers, the lips I have kissed and the hands held, the children I have made and sent out into the world. Thinking about him so much has made me feel more connected, yet it doesn't feel like a connection with the past; it feels like a connection to a boy who lives here and now, just over there.

I kneel next to the little beds I've made near the house and break up the soil with the hand-fork whose handle and tines have worn and polished smooth across the years, to fit the shape of my hand and the angle that I push it into the earth. Nobody else has ever used this fork; it would feel weird in somebody else's hand and I would briefly feel jealous, then silly at feeling jealous. When the soil is fragmented and fine, I push my finger in to make a hole and drop a pair of seeds in it, as I have done 10,000 times. Kneeling, I fade to boy and back to man, to boy to man to boy again, as we both kneel at a plot of earth with a hand-fork, sowing seeds. The same person, but out of phase. We make the same shape with arms and back and knees, do the very same task in the same state of mind. We click/lock into place together—a feeling that startles me and instantly breaks the connection. That felt extremely weird.

There are big round honesty seeds in my hand and, kneeling, I sow them in the earth. He didn't grow flowers, I think, I don't remember any; only vegetables, perhaps a few calendula to keep the blackfly off the beans, perhaps . . . perhaps? But as I draw that picture in my head to see if a memory comes and fits, the boy comes again and releases from the dark subconscious memory a different image. The ghost of his small hands where my big hands are, peeling seed cases off honesty. His mother had shown him how, handling these very seeds—and bringing the dried seed heads into the house for her to put in a vase! But we don't click/lock into place again. I didn't like it and I push him away.

I plant foxgloves bought in pots. Two-year-olds and one-year-olds. Foxgloves are biennial, they grow one year and flower the next, so putting in older and younger ones at the same time mimics nature and means there will be flowers every year. I plant some ferns around the water barrel, and hostas in pots sit on the rim and hang over the water. Taking my time—there is no rush to do a day's work and earn my pay any more, I can just do this poetry for myself.

The little apple tree close to the house needs pruning, so I do that and I'm back in that world where I do these tasks with confidence and creative, mindless joy, without a thought or plan, and feel so much at home. Taking out dead branches, the split and diseased and those that crossed and rubbed, opening up the crown as I have done for decades, as humans have done for centuries. Plugged into history and future, a quiet story of passing time.

I wanted to make a garden where I could forget, but in reality every garden is a garden of remembrance. When we moved here I asked my children what they wanted in this garden. My daughter wanted a tree, my son a pond. I dug over the whole garden to let the air and rain into the sour-smelling soil, which had been unused and was full of compacted rubble. My son and I dug a hole with a spade and planted this tree that was smaller than him; he wanted to help, he stamped down the earth and heaved the heavy watering can, and spilled a sparkling stream at the base of the tiny tree that was no more than a stick. He skipped back, laughing, so that his feet didn't get wet, and asked how long it would take to grow. He helped me dig the pond, then discovered that he could ride a bike and rarely came back to the garden again—he had wanderlust, a traveller's blood, as I once had. He is a man now, with a child and a home of his own, and I eat the apples from the tree we planted. My daughter's now a woman who, when she was little, had her flocks of friends who are still her friends, who came, slept over, squealed into the night while I stayed awake with bleary eyes kept on the children, as they climbed the street trees in the early hours and fell asleep on the grass in pink netting tutus, plastic tiaras and fairy wings. The pond filled with a dozen or more naked Barbies.

GREY SQUIRRELS chase each other, along the fence tops and on all the flat surfaces, up and down and sideways, like children playing. Like my children played. Time goes round again. The sparrows are flying in pairs and groups and on their own from tree to tree, finding a little thing to nibble, having a chat, then flying off again to nibble something more, like old ladies flitting from café to market stall to newsagent's, all the time chattering with the people they pass, people they have known for years and grew up with: who has died, who has just had a baby, who was having an argument last night, who got drunk and didn't come home, who has got a new dog, who has been arrested. A single black fly hangs under a brown leaf mere inches from my face as I kneel to plant a buddleia; he is taking it all in and enjoying the morning sun, like me. We are companions not even planning our day, because we don't need to plan, because we have nothing to do that has to be done, because this gardening, in my own garden, is mine and for me and is slow.

A kiss,
beautiful scars

The sky has darkened over the past two days and dulled to mostly white, and with it the temperature has dropped and things that were about to flower have stopped to wait for rain and sun. He is eleven and, on leaving school one day, a girl he doesn't know runs up, kisses him quickly on the cheek and says, 'That's from her' and points at another girl.

By the time he has turned to look, the girl has run to her friends and is walking away with three other girls who have their heads together, looking back to see if he is looking at them. He has no idea which girl the kiss was from. He wonders if he is expected to follow them; he does not, cannot possibly know what the rules are—if he gets it wrong, he could be horribly embarrassed. The risk is too great and he carries on walking home. 'It was probably just a trick,' he thinks, to make a joke of him; girls do things like that.

The next day nothing happens, but on the third day after maths another girl comes up and says, 'Do you like her then?'

'Who?' he asks.

She points to a girl and says, 'Alice.'

She is one of the clever girls, who behave and get on with their work, so are allowed to sit together at the back. She is pretty and small and catches his eye, then quickly looks away. The boy feels warmth inside, discomfort, excitement. He likes her, he does: he does like her. In truth, if anybody had said they liked him, he would have liked them back, he would have fallen in love. He can still remember the feel on his cheek of the girl who kissed him, and he likes looking at her too.

The girl who has spoken skips off and giggles, head together with her friends, who hang out in the corridor to see what happens next. The boy goes outside and stands by the wall across from the door and waits, standing, then leaning, then standing again, as he tries to look 'normal'. Alice comes out and glances, then turns and carries on walking neatly alone, her friends behind chatting and look-ing, directing with their eyes, mouthing at him, 'Go on then!'

Slow to catch on, but eventually he gets that he is sup-posed to catch up with her and nervously does, in case it's a trick, and walks next to Alice, matching her speed, feeling stressed and manipulated and worried.

'Hello,' he says.

'Hello.'

He tells her his name.

'I know,' she says. 'I'm Alice.'

'I know. Are you going home?'

'Yes.'

'Me too,' he says. 'Where do you live?'

'I live near the park. My dad picks me up in the car.'

'Oh, I walk home.'

As they walk out, she spots her dad in his car and says, 'See you tomorrow.' And that is it; as banal as it is, he has a girlfriend. He barely sleeps that night.

Alice. He thinks about her intelligent voice and the clear and hissy way she sounds every letter 's': Ali*sse*, ye*ss*, pick*ss*, *Ss*ee you tomorrow. He pictures her crisp, clean; her blue eyes, her short blonde hair, bobbed; her neat small mouth, pink lips. She is a nice clean person, she comes from nice clean people. Clean. He wishes he had held her hand, wishes that he had kissed her. Some of the boys would have done that already, he imagines.

At home he tries to draw her, sketching out in pencil her face, her hair, her eyes, and writes her name beneath it, then quickly tears it into pieces in case anyone should find it. He draws her again and again so that he can look at her. He struggles with eyes and nose and mouth; they will not look real or rest on her face, instead appearing to float in space above an oval moon. Frustration, a tightness in his chest, a tightness about his shoulders and neck that he cannot make his hands draw what he wants to see.

The following day is Friday and they meet in the school playground.

'There'*ss* a garden party at the church on *Ss*aturday, would you like to go?' she asks. 'The ticket*ss* are fifty pen*c*e.' (With an '*s*'.) 'We could meet out*ss*ide the church,' she says, 'becau*ss*e my dad will be dropping me off.' And he says 'Ye*ss*', accidentally copying the way she speaks, and 'I'll meet you there.' And he pecks her on the cheek and is allowed, and he feels brave and good and excited, happy and strangely different.

He has no idea on earth what a 'garden party' is, but nevertheless after school he asks his mum for fifty pen*ss*e and she says, 'Ask your dad', so he asks the Angry Dog, and the Angry Dog barks, 'What for?' and the boy tells him and the Angry Dog says, 'No' and 'You are not going' and 'I don't see why I should work all weekend and you go off spending my money and giving it to the church. You can stay home and help your mum. Do some of your drawings.'

On Monday at school, Alice ignores him.

'I'm sorry—look, I've done a drawing of you.'

She looks at it without expression.

He is ashamed and says, 'My dad wouldn't let me go.' The words fall from his lips like stones; each one makes him feel more ashamed, more angry, and he feels like a coward.

'I waited for you,' she says and walks upright away, so clean.

After that Alice ignores him, and before long she is seen holding hands with one of the more confident, cocky boys, a clean boy—one of the normal boys who play football. She suddenly seems more beautiful. They look at him across the playground and laugh. He knows they are laughing about his crappy drawing and its stupid floating nose, and she suddenly seems not very beautiful at all.

IN A SHORT TIME the boy does the wrong thing again. His feelings must have leaked out and the Angry Dog snarls, 'You will apologise for that.'

The boy has no idea what he has done that he needs to apologise for. 'Why? What have I done?'

'You know what you have done—now apologise.'

'How can I apologise for something if I don't know what it is?' he asks. He really does not know what he has done or said wrong, and it only makes sense that he should know what he has to be sorry about, so that he can genuinely be sorry about it. Eventually he will realise that he just doesn't understand what people mean or want most of the time.

'Outside, NOW!' growls the Dog and pushes the boy into the garden from behind, then a harder push and he falls into the rhubarb, flattening some stems, and wonders if he might be punished for that too. 'You are a worthless piece of shit, boy. What are you?'

He knows the routine: the boy is supposed to say, 'I'm sorry, Dad, I'm a worthless piece of shit' (he's done it before), and the Dog will tell him not to do it again, or to act his age or some such thing, and he'll be satisfied and it will all be over. But this time the boy doesn't answer, but simply gets up again and stares at the Dog. He doesn't care what happens to him.

'What are you?'

Again the boy doesn't answer, and once more he is knocked down with a hard push, this time to his stomach, winding him. And he sees his brother sitting on the step, crying real tears—a brother who was never hit like this, who did what he was told and smiled when it was expected of him and never answered back—and the flash of hatred is not for the father who beat him, for he is merely a trained animal who cannot help himself; the hatred is for the brother, who is clever and sneaky and has, in all probability, been the one who has done whatever it is that needs apologising for.

'Stay down, stay down,' his brother mouths.

But he gets up and looks his brother in the eye, with tears running down his face. Gasping for breath, he steps back onto something, turns and grabs the dried and heavy old piece of wood that has treacherously nearly tripped him over, the handle of a broken pickaxe that was under the rhubarb patch.

The Dog looks at him, looks at the club that the boy is holding and reads in his eyes that he will swing it, break open his head and release all the bad thoughts from his skull, to dissipate like a flock of gulls. He turns around to go inside, hurt and confused. It is a fight to the death of their relationship and, like two disagreeable farmyard dogs, they decide to keep their distance.

WHEN HE FEELS like crying, he sings through his tears and usually ends up laughing at the stupidity of it all, and sometimes when he cries he wraps his arms around himself and holds himself like a baby, whispering, 'Shhh, shhh, shhh' until he falls asleep.

Each little thing is perfect when it first emerges, perfect but easily damaged. The things a child learns cut deep, and all learning leaves scars that never completely go away— they are tough and beautiful; scars are self-repairing and more resilient than any unaffected part, stronger, firmer, and they give us our unique shape. Ask any tree—none of us are perfect specimens, and we all learn constantly from our environment.

THE BOY FELT SAD because he was worthless, and that was a bad thing. He holds himself and whispers, 'Shhh', into the night, and soon all he can hear his mind say is 'Shhh', instead of spinning and circling around and feeling shame or anger or sadness. There is no shiny answer, sparkling in the darkness. Soon all that exists is holding himself and whispering, 'Shhh'. The sound falls like rain, like cool air on his skin that makes him feel sleepy and at peace.

The rain comes and then passes, and sun comes again. He picks wolfsbane and rhubarb leaves and stores them in a coffee jar, where they slowly rot down into a foul-smelling poisonous black paste, into which he pours his hatred and all the magic he can muster, which he will use to kill the Angry Dog.

In his little plot, pairs of small leaves in rows have appeared, tiny and perfect and there on their own, so fresh, so new and growing like it is the most natural thing in the world. The tiny brown radish seeds he'd sown, which miraculously still held life after being found in a dusty drawer in an abandoned shed, swelled and opened and made a root and a pair of leaves. With his fingertips, which are becoming the strong and grubby fingers of a gardener, he pulls out the things that aren't growing in rows—the ones he didn't sow—and in just a few weeks his radishes grow another set of leaves, larger and wrinkly, with a few little holes where the slugs or something else has nibbled.

GARDENER

Feelings, desire and suffering, a concert

The boy felt anger, sadness, alone, a 'worthless piece of shit'. The words his father had slashed him with had stung for many years.

Our feelings come from stories that we tell ourselves. The asters on my desktop, bright and playful, simple, good, and in the same vase funereal ranunculus and iris—seriously purple, they remind me of a lover's dress. All the flowers' melancholic fading signals the brevity of life and shouts to me, 'Blossom while you can, you fool!' A mass of complex feelings, yet these blooms know nothing of joy or funerals or lovers' dresses, they are merely coagulated genes like us, evolved to survive and pass themselves on. They have no inherent joy or melancholy. Our emotions—all the things we ever feel—are personal judgements of value. The tinnitus that screams in my head is no more or less natural than birdsong, has no value beyond that which I give it. That worthless boy was some years later homeless for a while but, as he walked in his wilderness from bracken bed to sleepy woodland bower, his thoughts went something like this:

'If I am worthless, then I will find the world worthless too, for creating things like me that are worthless—if the world is worthless, then everything is worthless—if everything is worthless, everything is equal—if everything is equal, there is no such thing as worth or worthlessness.' Finally he thought, 'There is no such thing as worth or worthlessness, other than what my mind gives a thing.'

At this, his mind went silent. The scar of worthlessness had turned to gold and gave him strength, and became a word describing nothing more than the bark of a nervous dog.

Now the logic may be flawed, but it worked. Everything is flawed; if it wasn't, there would be no universe, because mutations and oddities are the events that make things happen. Perfection is simply an idea in a mind that doesn't exist in reality; there is not a straight line in the universe, even the planets are only roughly spherical; gravity and time shift and bobble all over the place. If something works, it works—flawed and imperfect, or not.

THE CHERRY TREE is about to blossom, pink tips show through tight green buds and I hear the breeze as it bounces through the springing knotty branches. This is no story, it has no value; this just is as it is, now and at peace.

Peggy comes down from her room where she writes. I smile at her. So thankful that she still smiles back after more than thirty years. I tell her I love her and that we are going to the The Bayleaf for a curry because I am too tired to cook. We eat salty food, drink too much cheap wine, and later I shower, wrap myself in a towel and we settle to look at the garden. She reads while a light rain splashes on the bricks. I accompany its small white hiss with Irish jigs on my mandolin. I am not a good player—amateurish, lumpy, repetitive and interrupted—but the cat doesn't seem to mind; he climbs into the velvet lining of my mandolin case. I can't play much but gentle trills, triplets and rolls and try to make them sweet—it's enough. The cat is curled and sleeping, and Peggy reads while the boiling milky-black sky becomes heavy and turbulent. The wind huffs and howls, and trees bend and leaves flap, and magpies bunched on branches ride their bucking whips. The rain comes straight down and fine, yet dense like silky hair that's blonde and thin, and then it's sideways and thick and splatters on the glass, and tiny lenses bend the light so that the lilac tree is caught in miniature in every drop. Imagination tells me those drops should be round, but they are all kinds of shapes, catching light from the yellow sky and turning it to black and white.

A web on the outside of the window has been there for over a week, stretched between the white-painted wooden bars in the corner of the window frame. When it first arrived I watched the spider build the spirals, then settle in the middle. Now it's tattered and just the long supporting strands remain. I imagine these to be the toughest part and maybe, if I'm lucky, the spider will return and I'll be here to watch it build its trap again.

A rumble in the distance—timpani on a darkened stage announce a performance. The audience goes quiet, the lights dim, ears prick up, hairs stand on end on arms and neck, another lighter rumble closer, then a flash, a crack across the sky, across the ears, across the air, which makes my arm hairs fizzle, and heavier droplets splash concentric circles in the milky water-butt until they meet and interfere; a pattern of waves rises and falls, then more drops that tap at different rates and thicken, the waves make interference patterns, then become more complex and chaotic and I cannot see a pattern any more. A curtain drops with noise that hisses on the new brick path, which, muddied from my making, is now being sluiced clean. A river soon flows along the bricks, not draining any more, runs down the gentle slope towards the bottom of the garden and makes pools to show the dips in the path that I thought I'd made so very flat.

Another rumble and a crackle, briefly lighting up the trees caught in the act of swinging. Off the shed roof a thin sheet runs; ripples mirror the undulations in the boards beneath and warp the greys of the reflected sky, then hang from the eaves in larger and larger drops that join together, become a silver edge, a wavy blade that falls and breaks like glass that's dropped and shatters. The foxgloves turn to face the ground, like children at a wedding ducking away from fists of rice thrown by laughing guests.

From the gutter on the roof three storeys up a quickly falling, slowly twisting plaited rope hangs and crashes in the puddle that it's made, and bounces up again and sparkles with reflected light, while at the other end, which must be slightly higher up, the gutter drips, plop-plop-plop, a rhythmic metronomic beat that's like a drummer on a galley ship that sails us through this storm. The orchestra rings and taps and tinkles on stone and glass and puddle, then begins to slow, as if the batteries are flat, the spring is winding down, the baton calms, the percussion slows to a patter and the drummer gently brushes and then stops. A crack in the sky. Some blue. Some sun to turn it all to steam and wind the mainspring up again. The foxgloves drip this precious stuff, and sparrows flit from pyracanthas to the holly and they sing.

Growing vegetables, a lost box

Shhh, the boy falls asleep listening to far-off coal trains rattling heavily through the night, the distant sounds of whistling diesel turbines and clanking wagons held low to the ground by cooler air. In the morning he picks peas, sits on the step of his shed and pods them, eating them raw, throwing the pods into the rhubarb 'for compost'. He saves a handful of the bigger peas to plant next year, puts them on the window ledge to dry and roll around his bench top for a while. This sunny day he's weeding between his rows of kale and radishes, and lettuce that's been eaten to rags by slugs; he pulls a couple of radishes out and nibbles without washing them, throwing the tops in the rhubarb too and sprinkling new radish seeds in the gaps from the packet in his pocket, exactly like the instructions on the back of the little envelope told him to. They grew!

Somehow when he's here, sitting in the dirt, his sadness falls away and he wants to sing, or just be really quiet and make the plot with its rows of plants look beautiful. Perhaps next year he'll grow some flowers and potatoes, and onions maybe? He needs a gardening book to learn how to grow things and, as his mum comes out, he asks her, 'Mum, can I grow more vegetables to eat, and flowers? Can you get me some seeds?'

His mother, hanging washing yet again, goes quiet for a moment, then finds the strength to tell her sad and happy boy that they are moving house.

'Did we tell you that we're moving house?' she says.

He looks up, startled rigid, and then, 'Oh, Mum, why?' And 'Bloody fucking shitting hell!'

'Hey, language!' Holding back a snigger at his profanity. Between the wooden clothes pegs in her mouth she says, 'You'll like it, we're going to the seaside.'

A few days later a vanload of wooden tea chests arrives, plywood boxes about three feet square that smell of tea and have Chinese characters printed on them, which remind him of the ladies in his encyclopaedia with baskets on their backs, collecting leaves. All their pots and pans and bits of stuff are packed away. He is given a box of his own and told to write his name on the side. He puts his books in the bottom, next to the bottle of poisonous black paste that he's going to kill the Angry Dog with, and his pencils and paints and drawing books, his tools and bits of wire, a clock he'd taken apart, the unused camera his uncle gave him and his little brown plastic transistor radio. He is told to put his clothes in carrier bags, and a few days later the removal van comes and everything is loaded in by men in brown overalls, and they all get into the Angry Dog's car and follow the van to Blackpool.

They pull up outside a house in a street of big houses that have names like Birch Villa and Park Hotel and The Beachcomber. Their house is called Beech Villa. The guest-house his parents are going to run is closed for the winter, and so he and his brothers each choose a bedroom that they can occupy while the building is prepared. In the 'summer season', as his parents begin calling it, the boys will have to share so that the rooms can be let out to paying guests, but for now the boy takes bedroom number nine, which is right at the top of the house, with a sloping ceiling and a skylight through which he can watch the gulls and clouds go by while he lies in bed. His brothers take rooms next to each other on the first floor, so he is two empty floors away and can have peace and space, away from noise and people.

The delivery men take the bags and packing cases from the van and they are stacked in the hallway. Over the next few days the boxes are moved to their various places around the house. The boy cannot find his box of stuff. He asks his mum if she knows where it is, then his brothers, but nobody has seen it and finally he asks the Angry Dog, who yaps, 'I haven't seen it—it was full of junk anyway.'

The last phrase is a dead giveaway; the boy feels a wave of hatred that takes a long time to settle, and the poison that fermented in its jar seems magically transferred right into his chest. Over the next few months the Dog from time to time will ask if the boy has any sticky tape, a felt pen, some scissors, a stapler, a pair of pliers, notepaper, a ruler, an extension cable, some wire, for the boy is the guardian of such things as are usually kept in a particular kitchen drawer. He takes great delight in looking his black poison directly at the Dog's mean eyes and saying, 'No, I haven't. I did have one, but it was in my box.' The Angry Dog will then wander off sheepishly with his head down and without his usual yapping.

The house has a yard with crumbling tarmac, where the guests will park their cars when they come. (His parents are using words he has never heard them use before: 'Guests, full-board, half-board, B&B, vacancies & no vacancies, tariff, commercial travellers.') There is no garden attached to the house, there are no plants beyond the weeds that grow in the gritty corners between walls and tarmac, no snails, no slugs. There are ants, both red and black, and crows and the smell of the sea and clean cool air and seagulls screeching, and he is allowed out on his own.

The beach is seven miles long, with trams running along the promenade from a fishing village at one end to a smart retirement resort at the other; in between is a promenade that in the autumn is illuminated at night with a million animated bulbs that flicker and dance, and with giant lanterns made of fibreglass in the shape of clowns and dancers. There's a permanent fairground, a tower, a zoo, a ballroom and dozens of tiny kiosks advertising a mermaid, a man who could eat a bicycle, a goat with two heads, a severed hand, a tattooed man. There are bingo stalls, seaside rock, and three fortune-tellers, all called 'Gipsy Rose Lee'.

There are three piers reaching into the sea, with theatres on them and famous comedians he has seen on television. The books that gave him his power are gone, and he's abandoned his garden island where he reigned, but has walked into a living encyclopaedia and is no longer outside, looking in.

GARDENER

Free will, choices,
Paradise Lost

BEES ON THE
ANGELICA

It's cold outside, but I have a book and a red woollen blanket that Peggy bought me from a mill that weaves near where she grew up, from fleeces that walk black-legged on the hills above. It's all very *Death in Venice*. Peggy brings washing down the new path that shines with small puddles to peg it on the line. I give her a hand and we hang my blue trousers, two white shirts, orange pyjamas, a yellow dress, underwear and socks. This bunting in front of the lilac tree and the little garden shed somehow makes it feel complete, an ordinary everyday home for me and Peggy and the plants and creatures we share it with. Somewhere deep inside, I'm still a painter of a sort and draw with my eyes the outline and splotches of colour of our familiar clothes that we inhabit day after day, which wrap and hold us tighter as the years go by.

My books give me power and I'm reading Milton's *Paradise Lost*, an epic poem about free will. It drops to my lap from time to time while I look mindlessly at my own paradise. The fresh air and its buzzing tug my sleeve and my attention away from the words. Mosses have already begun to grow in the joins of the new brick path; sunlight pours through leaves and makes moving patches of light on the bricks and ferns and foxgloves at its edge. To the left are shady stands of leafy angelica next to ferny dill, whose flat heads of flowers, when they come, will draw hoverflies in the heat and small birds in the winter. Under the branches, between the ferns, wood pigeons, magpies, robins and wrens. Blackbirds, sparrows and blue tits visit the barrel to drink from the rim, and hop through the old logs for woodlice and slugs and bits of twig for nesting. There is nothing to do but watch, let the world flow by and then wander in, to a do a few small things when the opportunity, or the need, arises. I need go nowhere. My van hasn't moved for six weeks.

It's warm and bright, hoverflies are hanging in the air and looking at the bluebells. Masses of tiny flying things hatch from the pool and congregate under the drooping bunches of lilac flowers that scent the warm air in waves, as barely moving breezes float their perfumed oils this way and that. Sparrows feast. It's April. Frantic wood pigeons call on the fence. Seagulls scream and wheel. The apple tree is budding and the walnut buds, still tight, are showing white and eagerness to burst. The cherry blossom in my little garden at the front is fully open and is loosening its grip already. Little tissue circles, plucked by breezes from the twigs, drift by as if a pigeon has fluffed itself on the roof and lost some down. The pink propellers of clematis will soon open and dangle in my garden from next door's holly tree. The wild garlic is releasing its earthy, oily, erotic scent; garden birds gather twigs and forage between the ferns. And somehow it's now lunchtime and I'm still sitting here.

Making the garden has slimmed me down and loosened my joints and increased my energy. It's getting warm and I want to soak my body under the sun—a jug of wine, a loaf of bread, tomatoes and cheese—and fill my senses with wilderness.

THE IDEA TO become a gardener all those years ago resolved itself when an old lady I knew needed someone to prune a fuchsia that was close to blocking her doorway. I had a vegetable garden of my own, an allotment rented from the council, and tools, so I did it for her. I didn't plan it to go this way. I responded to the environment like a sea urchin responds to touch. Nothing happens without a cause. Instead of taking control of my bit of the world, I had for some years been letting the world guide me, not resisting or paddling against the tide—taking care of myself and others, of my bit of the planet, but aware that I am not in charge, trying to be mindful of my part in the world when I could, when I remembered to pay attention.

Peggy and I were cruising to the west coast for a day at the sea in our ancient four-door Volkswagen and it was sagging desperately—I needed to earn a living. A road trip always solves a lot of problems, and sometimes we decide to take a long one simply because we have some creative issue that we need to sort out. Peggy said, 'You should be a gardener—you are always saying that you want to work outdoors.' And it felt like all the bricks tumbled down and made a home. I hadn't been paying attention at all, I'd never even thought of gardening for a living. I wasn't sure it could be done. I was writing, but nothing good was happening with that, and I'd been made redundant from my job as the editor of a little magazine that failed. I was unemployed. I'd worked in various jobs: as a graphic designer in a print shop and teaching art in a prison, and various other things that were far from suitable for somebody who questioned the rules as a matter of course and refused to be told what to do. The people I had to work with made me crazy, so I made some leaflets on my computer and walked the streets, sticking them through letter boxes.

By the end of a week I had enough gardening work to pay the bills, by the end of a month I was working full-time and turning work down, and in six months I was driving a van full of brand-new tools to the same wonderful humans every week. I sacked any customers who paid slowly or haggled. I walked off jobs where people were impolite or had unpleasant attitudes. I wouldn't work for anybody who had a dog that soiled in the garden. I ended up working for, and with, the loveliest people I could wish for, in gardens that I enjoyed. The days and months and years went by and my beard grew whiter and thicker. Eventually I worked in just one big garden every day through summer and winter for one lady: she at one end in the house, working with telephones, newspapers and screens, and I working outside with secateurs and plants and bees. She had the money and I had the freedom.

I already knew a fair bit about growing things because I had been growing fruits and vegetables for years and had studied with fingers and books, magnifying glasses and a microscope, and drawing in detail since I was a boy the soil and plants and the tiny living things that make it work. But tending ornamental plants was new, so I bought and read lots of gardening books, encyclopaedias of plants and flowers, and seasonal guides and books about pruning and feeding and microbes and compost and lawns. A whole library of books about gardens, from Japan to Babylon. I like to learn and teach myself. I studied hard and talked to other gardeners, and learned what I needed to know, and more that I didn't need to know but enjoyed anyway. I was a pretty good gardener, I think.

Do we choose our path? Or is it all merely ripples that started like a raindrop falling in an infinite pool, and the universe exploding from nothingness thirteen billion years ago? Perhaps each of our thoughts go all the way back to then, and you and I are what we were always going to be, acting and reacting. Eton boys and farmers follow tracks laid out by generations past and cannot contemplate another way of life. The men in my family were soldiers and policemen and railwaymen. Everyone I knew, when I was a child, expected that I would follow them into a uniform and take up a weapon. No one I knew grew things; there were no artists or writers or readers in my family, nobody went to college. When I chose not to eat the animals, my family did not understand. It was news to them, it was news to me—I didn't think it through. I knew there was suffering and I didn't want to add to it; the animals and insects were my company and I developed empathy. There was no soul-searching or planning or thinking, I simply decided—or was it merely a response to a stimulus? This is unknowable and was the beginning of a lifelong view that every living thing has equal value.

When I meditate my physical boundaries are not so constrained—what is me and what is not-me are the same thing; in fact often there is no 'me' and no 'not-me', there just is. The birds that sing, the breeze that blows, the stream that trickles, the breath that moves are all part of the same thing, whatever that is. I experience this regularly and know it well. The animals that I choose not to eat are also part of this, and I feel that harming them was harming myself—whatever that 'self' was. Each dead animal hurt me in a subtle way, diminished and changed me, took away a little sensitivity, which I had to work hard to regain.

We cannot know any more about a thing than what it does and what it is made of. I am what I do, we are all what we do: nothing more than the sum of our actions. I take things easy, I work, eat and rest—nothing special, ordinary. I'm liberated from all that stuff, that passion, evaluation and self, fear and hate. When you don't fear dying, you stop caring so much about material stuff because you see that it, too, is only passing.

I'm reading Milton's epic poem of Satan, who escapes the fiery hell that God, for his arrogance, had chained him to. His battle with God, wars between angels and demons, his transformations into toad, then bird, then snake, and his temptation of Eve, who eats the fruit of self-awareness and is cast out of the Garden of Eden. Self-awareness means the loss of paradise in fiction, poetry and life, and I will happily keep this garden and not-knowing in exchange for any sense of being a separate self. We are an expression of nature that has become aware of itself and its inevitable demise. How we suffer, because of that awareness.

The book falls slowly to my lap and I watch a great tit peeling snakeskin bark from next door's acer tree; she comes back four more times, after flying below the washing line and around the close-cropped hedge to wherever she is making her nest. She is not choosing—just doing. Four wood pigeons blunder their lumpy way onto the roof and sit there, burbling and staring at me with their funny stupid faces; behind them, bubbly white clouds hang in the blue, the blackbird singing somewhere in another hedge until he breaks from his branches and flits across the garden. A sparrow in the budding lilac watches me as I watch him or her, neither of us moving, until the spell is broken and I turn, distracted by a grey squirrel, and the sparrow cheeps, then flies. This being here right now—this 'is', this very moment—is everything that's real. This 'is-ness' without knowledge is paradise and it was never lost, we merely became too self-important to see it. The gull high overhead turns towards the setting sun and its back turns rose-gold as it carves a curve beyond the trees and shrinks into the blue.

I could go inside and get warm, but I pour a whisky, then come out again, ignore the book and wrap the warm red blanket round me and look at the little plot. The foxgloves are open, the fat bees land on their lips, walk in to fill their panniers with pollen, then back out and bumble to the next one; the stems and buds are reaching up and everything is green and fresh.

Tea for three, Blackpool rock

The spring has turned into summer and the boy is free. Fire-eaters, jugglers, stilt-walkers, clowns and little people wander around the town handing out free tickets to the circus. The Angry Dog seems much calmer these days, almost cheerful, certainly too busy to pay attention to anybody else. In the first few days the boy goes out of the front door and explores his new domain. In the old place, the main roads at the end of his street went nowhere that a boy could safely go and his entire world consisted of school, the row of shops, his house and its back garden. At the end of this road there is a beach, and the sea. There is no sense of loss. He adapts. He feels now that he will survive and that here is a place he can do so. Sometimes all it takes to turn your feelings round is a change of location.

He sits at the top of the cellar steps in the sun, watching ants pour in and out of sandy cracks. He places a twig in their path to see what they do, and instead of going over the twig they appear confused; one of them climbs up and walks along it, with antennae twitching, stopping from time to time to rub its legs together, and another follows. Their world has changed, upset their plans, everything has fallen apart. Another walks along the ground to the end of the twig, then back again. Eventually they work it out, and the stream of ants goes over and round as they absorb the twig into their path. They go where they were planning to go, without bark or shout or tantrum; the obstacle simply slowed them down for a while as they figured out what was different and what they needed to do about it.

He wonders why are there ants at all? Why is there a him or his father, or mother or brothers, or a house or sea or world? 'It just goes on, and on,' he thinks, and if he stands on an ant by accident and it dies by accident, does it matter? Who would it matter to? The other ants? Would it matter if he died by accident? Perhaps, to one or two people, he thinks. Grandparents? Mother? Father? Brothers? But even if it mattered, it wouldn't matter for very long. They would be sad and would remember something that was not his life, but their version of it and, like the ants, they would absorb their changed world and get themselves back on track and carry on.

He could stand on an ant and kill it and see what happened, but it would matter to him if he killed one, even by accident. He would not kill an ant, and he squats and wonders why. He imagines it would matter more to him than it would to the ants. Perhaps the other ants wouldn't even notice; then he remembers them bringing their babies out into the sun and he thinks perhaps they would. But it would mean something about himself. He would feel mean and unpleasant, dismal, because he had chosen to be unkind for no decent reason at all. He would feel that he was like his father. Why would someone choose to be unkind? He's seen boys being cruel to each other, to insects, worms and cats, for fun, and wonders why. The world is cruel enough; why would they enjoy adding to it?

He wonders if the ants think and, if they do, do they all think the same thing at the same time? Do they ever feel lonely? If he takes an ant away from the others, puts it in another part of the yard, will it find its way back or will it start to live alone? He could take one away and see what it does. But he would feel like the God he no longer believes in, playing games with other lives for fun. He thinks of Slow, the slug, and wonders if he damaged its life by taking it off and putting it in a jar, but imagines that slugs are not very family-oriented creatures; they don't wander about in herds like the ants and the sparrows, they are more like cats and seem to prefer to be alone, like him. And anyway he put Slow back where he found him—he'd only been away for a week, on holiday.

Sitting on the step in the sun with his back against the bricks, he tries to see himself in the ants, but now he sees himself in the behaviour of slugs and cats and suddenly feels fine. 'I'm like them,' he thinks and looks at the sky, where a solitary crow flies by, and feels good and not like the lonely ant cut off from its tribe; he is not a creature of a tribe. Some people are like dogs and enjoy being with other people, and some people are like cats and like to be on their own, and that he thinks is fine.

It is the nature of some children that their thoughts go deep, but move on fast—this is a gift that nature gives the powerless—but thoughts when they pass leave a feeling behind, and he's quizzical. Soon another feeling comes to replace it, the feeling that everything is going to be okay or at least it will be interesting; perhaps everything is always okay, perhaps it doesn't matter if it is or not. He wanders down the empty yard, where cars will soon be parked, between the shoulder-high brick walls to the black-painted double gate at the end, and he opens it to see what's there and goes out into a back lane.

There are children playing in the lane, who stop and turn to look at this kid just arrived. A short-haired girl in a sundress and sandals on a blue bicycle with tassels on the handlebars tears past him down the alley; two running boys are racing her, trying to keep up. Two little girls younger than him sit on the cobbles outside the row of garages, with a plastic tea set. 'Hello, hello,' they say; and, shy, he says his hello back, and a tender girl with pink spectacles and grubby knees pours nothing from a plastic teapot into a tiny, dirty, yellow plastic cup and offers it to him on its saucer; and, bigger and much older than either of them, he sits cross-legged on the dusty cobbles and joins in their game, and they look as poor and as dirty as he.

'Have you got any money?' one of them asks.

He shakes his head.

'Never mind,' she says. 'I have—let's go and get some rock.'

They want to show the new boy around and tend to him. He is bigger than them, like a cuckoo, but they get up and leave the tea set there, the cups all fallen over, and they walk down the lane together, exchanging names.

'Are you new?'

'I suppose so. I've just moved in.'

'Where did you come from?' And conversations like grown-ups have.

They start to run, so he runs too, to the end of the lane, past the girl on the bike who's racing back, and now she seems to be a boy and he slows down to look at her as she, or he, speeds past, and he feels a tingling of excitement. They will become lovers of a childish sort for a while.

The girls and the boy arrive at a massive blue wooden door on rollers that's slid all the way open, to let out the heat that comes from two shiny steel cauldrons that steam at the back. There's a long metal table where men and women dressed in white, with hair-nets and gloves, roll a stick of rock that must be fifteen feet long and chop it into shorter sticks with massive scissors. The smell of hot sugar and peppermint and humbug fills the air.

The girls walk straight into the factory. He follows cautiously, restrained by the fear of doing something wrong, past a machine the size of a wardrobe, with metal arms that weave around in a figure-of-eight. The mindless, powerful robot arms are stretching and pulling a tangle of melted sugar. At the far end of the table a big pink lump of sea-side rock, about a foot across, rotates on a pair of metal rollers. It's hot, and men are rolling and pulling and drawing it out down the table; at the end where it's thinner and cool, the woman with scissors snips it into foot-long sticks. Everything is hot, with the sweet smell of sugar and peppermint. On a wall is a handwritten sign on a piece of brown cardboard that says, 'Pilfering means instant dismissal.' He doesn't know the word 'pilfering' and wonders if it is literally just another word for 'instant dismissal', but he doesn't know what 'instant dismissal' means, either. Below the sign is a table with a dozen or more white-paper sweet bags filled with broken pieces of rock.

A man comes down and says, 'What can I get you girls?'

'A bag of broken rock, please,' says the girl with the money.

She gives the man a two-pence piece, which he puts in a tin and hands her a bag of bits of rock, mixed flavours of striped fruit rock, pink peppermint and brown-striped humbug, some of them still warm and chewy.

'They are bits off the ends of the sticks,' she tells the boy, 'that's why they're all squashed in.'

And he takes a piece of humbug rock that says inside, 'Niagara Falls'.

They wander out and stand at the doorway, chewing and watching a man make letters from slabs of clear boiled sugar coloured red; he makes a letter L and lays it flat on a slab of white rock, next to the B, L, A, C, K, P, O and O.

The empty spaces in and around the letters are filled in with white rock, more letters are added and another slab of rock goes on the top, and then the whole thing is rolled around until the words BLACKPOOL ROCK are a circle inside.

Over the weeks of summer the boy's world becomes—instead of being alone in the garden with books and plants—a back alley filled with the children of hoteliers, circus performers, singers and artistes, a rock factory, and little girls and a boy who's both a boy and a girl, and ordinary boys who play football up and down the street. He has friends. He feels a happiness that has a very different flavour from his happiness before: a sweet and minty flavour.

GARDENER

Witness, enjoying
the movie, hedgehogs

❊ ❀ ❊ ❀

Lying in bed, Peggy says, 'I wish you weren't older than me. I love you. I don't want you to die.'

I make up a story for her that goes like this:

'Eventually I'll be really old and lose my eyesight,' I say, 'and because I'm wrinkly and a bit crap, you'll take a lover—I think he's called Paul. And one sunny day you'll help me find my shorts because I can't see them, because my eyesight is going, then you'll help me to step into them, one skinny leg at a time, pull them up and tie the string and you'll take me for a day out on the beach, but Paul—your lover—will be waiting there already, and you and Paul will hide behind a rock and laugh at me stumbling about the beach, shouting, "Peggy, Peggy, where are you my love?" with my hands outstretched.'

I sit up in bed, close my eyes to show her, and wave my hands about in front of me, in a stupid parody of a blind person.

'While you and Paul are behind the rock, laughing like toddlers and saying, "Look at the stupid old man, he's going for a swim", I fall over a mollusc, and you two laugh even harder and have to put your hands over your mouths, so that I don't hear you as I cry for help. "Help me, Peggy," I shout, "are you there?" And you start to feel a bit sorry for me as I crawl along in the surf, crying. I can't tell where the land is, because I have gone deaf as well by now, and you and Paul stand up on the rock to watch. The last you see of me, I am lying face-down in the sea with my hands flapping a bit finny, and you turn to Paul your lover and say, "It is what he would have wanted."'

Peggy is laughing at my story and has to run to the toilet so that she doesn't wet herself. I'm not that much older than she is anyway—nine years, eight for a while, after her birthday, until mine comes around, and then it's nine again.

When she comes back I say to her, 'Life is absurd, it's like a movie; it doesn't mean anything, it isn't a sign or a clue to something else, it is just what it appears to be. We come in and watch it, and are part of it, and then we leave and become part of something else. You wouldn't go to a movie and spend your time thinking about what you had done before you got there, or what you were going to do when you leave. You would sit and watch it, and absorb and enjoy every moment of it as if it were real. That is what life is like,' I say. 'Sometimes it's scary and sometimes it's fun, and sometimes you might even wish it would end. So don't worry about the ending, that'll come in its own time—enjoy the movie! There will be sadness, that is the price we pay for love, but we can deal with all that later, when it's time.'

This body is not yours, it is nature's. This mind that calls this body yours is not your mind, it belongs to nature. None of this is you or yours, it is all nature expressing itself; there is no 'you' that is anything more than nature—nature singing its wonderful song. It breathes you into the world, then out again, and you are just a single breath. All the things in nature arise, then fall: this is you.

None of it means anything until we make up a story or borrow someone else's and give it a meaning. The meaning I give to life is love. This is just my point of view. Attachment to any particular way of viewing the world is rarely helpful to a living thing; it isn't real and it pins you down and fixes you in place, while the nature of life moves along. Without uncertainty there is no growth, so I'm happy to be changing and uncertain, but I try to hang on to love through it all, because that is my folly and it's fun.

THIS TINY GARDEN on the edge of town is full of life: the pile of rotting logs is alive with slugs and woodlice and beetles and fungus; the birds visit all day long, and hedgehogs in the night. I won't feed the wildlife unless it is in trouble. The garden feeds them naturally, and somehow they find this place among the sterile roads and gardens of concrete and decking and mown grass. Animals suffer because of our desire. If I drive my van, I am responsible for the pollution; if I cut the grass, I am responsible for the bees; if I spray the roses, I am responsible for the birds; if I fly in a plane, I am responsible. I may be an expression of nature, but I do have some choices. Every little thing we do has a consequence, and all those little streams of consequence will run and grow for decades and become an overwhelming torrent. So I do not mow, I do not spray, I do not fly and I drive as little as I can.

People encourage birds to visit gardens by putting out food that's not as varied as they would get in nature—they don't have to work or hunt or forage, so they get weak and diseased and cluster together and fight. Trichomonosis from bird-feeders has killed millions of garden birds and has cut our greenfinch population in half. And we have taken away the fields and woods full of seeds and fruits and bugs, so they find what they need to survive in our gardens and we make the planet sick through our desire.

There are young sparrows eating greenfly in the roses a yard or two away. One of these tiny, almost transparent creatures lands on my bare arm, it wanders along, struggles through my pale arm hairs, which are twice as thick as its jointed legs, and I imagine its tiny little knees as it probes for a path. What does it want of me? It cannot drink my sap, I cannot feed its young. I can barely feel it there and, just as quickly as it appeared, it is gone. The roses are open and full, and I love my life and this world and feel so deeply connected; my dusty bare feet on the ground are roots. It would be impossible to feel alone.

Elephants, powdered horses, half a lady, people from Glasgow

He is on the beach, smiling as if his face would crack in two, filled with breathless wonder and love and joy. There are circus elephants on the shore, having exercise and fun. He has never seen a real elephant before. The grey and dusty beasts are managed by handlers with long sticks, which they hook into the elephants' ears to draw their attention, changing their direction as if they were driving big, leathery cars. The elephants sit in the surf and have the smell of cage scrubbed off with brushes—they are enjoying themselves, raising their trunks and smiling! Their great glutinous eyes follow the boy as he stands and looks, amazed; they seem joyful, so cheerful to be there and sharing the beach with the smiling boy. Their wrinkly knees remind him of his grandmother's knees and stockings; she was tall and said to be 'big-boned'. In the distance he sees white circus horses too, which canter and then walk elegantly, their knees drawn high and their heads pulled back, then they splash and run in the water with their necks long and down. Their riders are urging the horses on into splashing gallops that wet their flanks and spray their riders' grinning faces.

The guesthouses each had a book of free circus tickets to give out to holidaymakers who would, it was supposed, bring their friends who'd pay for their own tickets. But there were always a few left over, and the boy goes to the circus three or four times a year and sees the same show every time, each visit revealing more of how it works.

At night the horses are powdered, made pure white again, and are ridden by slender girls in tutus and ballet shoes and costumes that look barely there, under spotlights that make the horses shine, crystalline like living chalk; and sequins and rhinestones sparkle and flash on the girls' white costumes. When he gets closer he sees that their flesh only pretends to be naked: the arms and legs, from cuff to ankle and neck, are tightly wrapped in thick stretchy fabric zipped at the back, the texture of fabric sticking plasters, the colour of a hard plastic doll. They are women who look like children. Under the piled-up hair, a face that smiles without breaking has a thickly painted grin that masks the concentration, which is hard-working, focused underneath. Their job is to make it look easy and fun. They sparkle and stand on the horses' backs and gallop around the ring to shouts of 'Hup! Hup! Hup!' as men hold hoops up high above the horses' heads for the women to jump through and land safely, with a puff of chalk dust on the thundering animals' backs.

From the cheap seats, the free tickets give him a view into the darkness of tunnels where the performers emerge and props are prepared. The clowns who tumble bright and playfully in the ring become working men with tired muscles when they leave the lights, brushing and powdering horses, organising the steel platforms for the elephants to stand on and the hoops for the jumping ladies; they throw the jugglers their clubs from the darkness to catch, as they spin like glitter into the spotlights above the freshly sawdusted ring. The chaos and fun rehearsed and tightly timed by hours of hard work and practice.

He watches the magician over and over again. The illusionist started as a wonder, but is soon revealed as a sneaky manipulator of cloths and fast fingers, and black-painted boxes where white rabbits crouch behind mirrors reflecting the darkness. The blonde lady in a ballgown sawn in half is two ladies who look the same. They are in fact the same two, now red-headed ladies, who uncurl themselves, outstretched and proud with pointed fingers and toes, in complete control of every single muscle and joint and bone in between, in sinuous snakelike outfits, from suitcases carried into the ring by a clown who pretends to be drunk and staggers off, leaving them in the spotlight. The boy wonders about this story and what kind of chap wanders through the night, presumably after an evening in the pub or at a party, with a suitcase full of snakes and then forgets them. The tumbling dwarves seem angry; the light-as-air girls are muscled women, the acrobats swarthy and aggressive; the smiles are masks over hard work and pain.

'It's all a show—everything is just a show,' the boy said to his mum.

'I know, love,' she said.

'The whole world is show business, designed to distract your attention from what's going on and take money off people who only want to have fun.'

'Yes, love, I know,' she said. She seemed happier now at the seaside, cooking for strangers who enjoyed what she did; in her clean cuffs and apron and tied-back hair, she glowed with appreciation.

'They only want your money,' he said to the guests in Beech Villa.

'I know,' they all said. 'And we're here to spend it!' They laughed.

He thought it was sordid, and imagined himself clever for figuring out what was going on, but they knew they were being conned and they were in high spirits, even gleeful to pay for it. They wanted glamour. They wanted to be distracted; they knew it wasn't real, didn't want yet more unhappy truth. That was why they came here. This was show business. Performer and audience were in the con together.

The holidaymakers were drawn to the jangling of shows and barking bingo-callers, the neon amusements, the booze, the sun, the beach, the fresh sea air and the scent of new relationships. They came from Scotland at first, on the train and wearing their Sunday suits and hats, and they walked with their bags through the town looking for their digs.

'Are you in Beech Villa with us?'

'No, we are next door in The Pines!'

When the people from Glasgow left two weeks later, people came from Yorkshire in a long line of coaches that parked on the prom, and then they came from Manchester, then Preston, then Oldham and Bolton, and every two weeks the town was washed by a tide of one accent, then another, and the shows reset to their starting positions and began again. The town itself was constantly changing, absorbing and adapting to be the place they wanted it to be as the cotton and wool mills, looms and steelworks of the North closed down for holidays. The workers together took trains or coaches to escape to the seaside with co-workers, families and friends, for fresh air and to let their hair down. They left the house noisily each morning after eating eggs and bacon, sausages, black pudding, toast and marmalade, cornflakes or porridge, depending on where they came from—all cooked by someone else for a change, and washed down with pot after enormous pot of tea.

In their best holiday clothes, they treated the town as a stage where they performed to attract ladies or men, also dressed in their best. They came here to be someone else for a while; they came to play, and they played and had fun and then left. The boy enjoys all the come-and-go, the high-spirited people, the perpetual holiday atmosphere, and finding friends who also bathe in colour and glamour, but he's torn; let's face it, he is dour and thinks the not-real is somehow wrong. The happiness is real enough on the faces of the people, but the things that make them happy are fake, frivolous and superficial. He is a bit judgy, but he's young, he is still looking for meaning and he hasn't found love yet.

Forget-me-nots, Zen monks, colour and scent

The garden is buzzing. I make soup with the wild garlic; a hedgehog comes to visit in the evening and scuffles in the litter by the log pile for the slugs and woodlice who've made a home there. I've rearranged some logs to make a gap that he or she might fill with leaves and spend a winter there. The firethorn's white spring flowers are gone and, in their place, green ovaries swell for winter birds who shelter from the local cats behind their lethal thorns.

There isn't much bare earth on show for weeds to grow, so if it isn't invasive, I leave it in for texture. Forget-me-nots with bright-blue flowers and shepherd's purse, the second most-common flowering plant on Earth, got here on their own and can spread where they will. I leave any leaves and fallen flowers on the earth and throw my prunings to the back of the garden, where they'll rot by the logs, where fungus, woodlice, slugs and worms will turn them back into soil. All I want to do is play and be spontaneous while the universe makes a work of art. Zen monks used to practise letting go of the self by trying to put dots of ink on a piece of paper without making any discernible pattern; the idea is to be spontaneous, without the controlling, organising mind. It is intensely difficult, yet the cherry drops her blossom and the lilac her leaves—they do it with ease, and I cannot see any pattern at all.

I find different ways to lose myself each moment of each day. Gardening, walking, cooking, polishing my shoes, putting dots on paper. When that self is lost there is a calm and endless sea of happiness—or call it love, or God if you want, they are the same thing.

I trained as a painter, immersed myself for years in art and the artist's life. I played with weight and balance, colour, harmony and line, light and shade. I still think of myself as a painter rather than a gardener or a writer. A painter with flowers and trees or a painter with words—it's all the same, it's just looking really. Paying attention. Painting is gardening, and writing is gardening; getting dressed in the morning and putting on a tie is gardening too; making tea, brushing my beard, putting flowers in a vase and chopping logs for the fire are gardening: all a playful loss of self. Using the senses of touch, smell, memory and taste to create something that leads the mind out of the head to this or that, or an interplay. Hiding things in the undergrowth for texture, the underpainting that only the creator knows, which builds the structure and mood and journey, a little dark or light or colour, mixing fantasies and truths and hiding one inside the other for people to find, for their entertainment and mine.

There are roses on the desk where I write. I grew them for Peggy, who loves yellow roses. Their scent fills the room, most thickly around me, and I pause between sentences to breathe in deep and carry on writing in a cloud of their perfume. The scent of their falling petals and the row of old books behind them together make something unique. Oh, sniff! Stop reading! Hold up this book and sniff these pages now and seek it out: the marzipan and frangipane, vanilla scents of new books, ice cream and softwood chips released by the moisture of your breath. Be a lover!

Turn down the volume of your thoughts, turn up your senses, lose yourself; pick up a brush and a bottle of ink, or seek to find and understand the most distant sound you can hear; or sniff the air to identify as many different scents as you can. Excuse me for a moment while I sniff this . . . what is it? Burning sugar from somewhere far away, but strong and sweet? Tea from the iron teapot by my side (lapsang), a bit of rust, what else? . . . wool, warm wool from my clothes and my body, and lilac coming all the way upstairs from the open back door . . . and that sweetness that I first thought was sugar is sandalwood, from my neck tie, where I was zapped by a woman at the Guerlain counter in town, weeks ago when I went shopping with Peggy. I am developing a bit of a thing for scents. I put my knitted tie to my nose and draw in fruity, woody aromas of frankincense, sandalwood and . . . could it be geranium?

When you leave yourself and then return, you find you are transformed; the biggest transformation is that you know that what you see as yourself is merely an illusion. You are far bigger than this meaty body and suffering, everyday mind that you occupy; you are, when you let go of that little 'self', everything and everybody that exists.

Winter, hand of glory, Gipsy Rose Lee leaves, rust

The boy walks to the sea and along the shore, scanning the seaweed and crabs and empty shells, and fishing floats and knots of nylon rope and net, and begins to feel that he belongs: not to family or to people hidden in their shells who feel they are entitled to control or benefit from him, but instead to salty waves and wind and sand and all their flowing tides. He lets this feeling go its way, abandons himself to its vagueness and wonder and—ashamed but unable to resist, unplanned, unthought, unpredictably, viscerally— in a moment of reaction, he kneels. Then lies. Face-down on the sand, and drives his arms as deep as they'll go into the beach, and holds it to his heart and whispers slowly with a pause between the words, 'I love you.'

He tries to understand, cannot see the point of choos- ing to have the real world hidden with glitter and gloss and live in a pretend one. How can that be a good life—a life separate from nature and its reality? He feels as if he is not supposed to be here in this world of people. As if he is all wrong somehow. Sometimes he cries. Avoiding eye contact, avoiding people, he walks alone for miles, from his house to the promenade, then north and at the end turns back south to the other end and then back home. He wonders what he should do in the world, why he is here.

Winter comes and the sea boils. The holidaymakers go back to their jobs. Clean cold air and wind blow through the strangely empty town, the promenade illuminations are switched off, the bingo booths and tourist shops closed down, the piers padlock their folding iron gates, the flashing lights, crackly music and recorded invitations from loudspeakers to 'roll up, roll up and see... the living mermaid swimming in a tank... the gory tattooed man banging nails into his face... the two-headed goat curled in a pickle jar... the severed hand of glory with its burning fingers' cease; and the jangling bells of slot machines go dark and silent behind chain-link shutters and peeling wooden storm-doors and flapping canvas tied with ropes to sandbags.

The sequinned huts of Gipsy Rose Lee have painted wooden boards fastened to their fronts, which cover up the faded photographs of different Roses reading palms or tarot cards or crystal balls for celebrities of decades past. A few small shops stay open, selling cigarettes and fizzy drinks, folding plastic macs and rain hoods, penknives and ball-point pens with pictures of ladies in them, who drop their clothes and show their breasts when you tip them over, to day-trippers who, if the weather is nice, come in cars at the weekends, but everything else is closed and boarded, and what was tacky and bright and cheaply fun shows its brittle surface gloss.

Beneath it lay a world of damage, its underside dark and real, with acres of nature's colours and textures of creased green tarp and splintered wood and cracking seaside paint that blended with the wet sand and the grey and boiling sea. It was real. He saw that it was all real, and all the sparkly stuff was harmless fun, entertainment, gloss and thrills, designed with joy to hide the scariness of reality, to make the world feel safe and protect us from its uncaring violence; it's all a kind of cosy nest that we build around ourselves to help us feel secure.

Darkness comes at 5 p.m. and he walks on the empty promenade, where he can see the Milky Way and distant lights of fishing boats. When the storms come, tons of sand and stones are washed into the road, and rusty old diggers and trucks trundle out from where they hide, and push it all back to the beach after the storms have passed; and tractors with giant steel rakes smooth it out before the holidaymakers return. Anything metal is rusty. The salty air chews its way through any thickness of paint—a little scratch will let the salt inside and turn the surface of the metal into rust. The paint will start to bubble, then eventually burst like a blister, to leave a bright-red rusty scab that will in the spring get painted over again and again, year upon year, layer over layer. The railings on the seawall are knobbly with scabs, like the branches of ancient oaks that eventually rot right through and burst; ripped open, they become dangerous iron blades that threaten to slash. They are cut off by men with goggles and gas torches, who replace them with shiny new lengths of pipe and paint it green, and for a while it looks too fresh and smooth and out of place, until nature gets her teeth in and starts to wrench it back.

He is happiest wrapped in thick clothes. Wrapped in solitude. In woolly jumpers, heavy shoes, wool trousers, a scarf and a waterproof coat. He walks in the rain alone and watches it splash into a calm sea, or shine on tram tracks and drip off light bulbs, to hear its hiss or plop, to feel the slippy sand gritting between his shoes and the path, to hear and feel its slide and crunch. He feels as solid and as real as the sea, as much a part of this place as the rust, as the splintered coloured bits of fishing boats that wash up on the shore and the knots of fishy smelling rope; as gulls, as shells, as rocks because . . . because he is silent and hears the world around him sing. He walks for miles and feels it sing, and remembers his garden and his books and losing them, and doesn't mind.

THE GUESTHOUSE never makes enough money to keep them through the winter and his father has to take jobs after the holidaymakers have left; he was a chauffeur one winter, and the next he played Father Christmas in a department store, which the boy thought was ironic. His mother is getting ill. The Dog is increasingly angry again. Once more there is no money. They have tried and tried and tried and have both worked their lives away at jobs, at failed businesses started on a shoestring. The rent is high, the guesthouse rates 'competitive' and the price of food and gas is going up. The boy once opened the toilet door and found the Angry Dog inside, sitting, smoking and crying his heart out; they just looked at each other, and the boy closed the door and walked away.

After four summers they move house again. The boy can't say goodbye to the kids in the street, as they don't come out in winter and have never been in each other's houses—their lives always out from under their parents' feet, on the beach or on the street or in the alley. Some are rich and live in hotels that their parents own, and they go away to winter somewhere warm, but most are poor and rent; and they, like him, are prone to come and go. Before they leave, he goes to see for one last time the promenade and the sea, and the piers with their glazed and sequinned arches that flash and twinkle in the breeze and light. He imagines he will never see this seaside town again, but he does; he will return and spend a night or two sleeping under the pier, watch jellyfish spawn in the dark, find a job for a while in a warehouse that ships plastic macs and ballpoint pens with ladies in them who show their breasts.

Paradise lost

A TALL THIN HOUSE / / /

WITH A
CHERRY TREE

I'm sitting in the garden reading and from the back door Peggy calls, 'I'm off to town, do you want anything?'

I ponder for a while and cannot think of anything that I would want.

'Well?' she says, as I'm thinking of asking for world peace, a Ducati motorcycle, a nice cold slice of flan, a Gipsy caravan and horse.

'No thanks, honey,' I answer. 'See you later.'

'See you later, love,' she says, then goes inside and shuts the door. I hear the tongue slide into the frame: it clicks and I'm locked out. I jump up—as much as I can jump up these days—and rush over to the door to call her, but as I get there I see through the window the front door close with a bang, and my phone on the kitchen table next to my mug of tea. Could I climb the six-foot fence, I wonder, into next door's garden and make my way through their bamboo and over their tall fence, too? Not a chance!

My neighbours have keys, but are both out, so all I can do is wait. I carry on reading, until I see the first few rain-drops splash on the page. It will pass, I think, and take my chair into the little shed, while big black clouds roll over and the sky darkens and the earth falls into shade and quiet, then the ferns begin to bounce as raindrops hit, and I listen to them strike the big heart-shaped leaves on the lilac tree, splat and splash into the water butt. I can hear each drop as it strikes, but the splat speeds up into a splatter, then patter, and then becomes a white-noise hiss and then a roaring blast of crashing waves, one after the other.

'Everything changes,' I say to myself as I stand in the doorway of my little shed and peer into the sky to see that there's not a bit of blue anywhere. There seemed a bit more space in here when I was little. 'The rain comes and then it passes,' I think, as I do so often, 'and then it comes again and stays around for a while and soaks me to the skin.' And I think, 'I like the rain' and then, 'You like it, don't you, Marc—you bloody love the rain, you keep going on about how much you love it.' I am cold and wet and miserable, so I go inside the shed, sit on the chair and watch the rain through the window and wait.

I've lived in this house for thirty-five years, and it has been an adventure. You emerge from the best of adventures with a completely new 'self', and this has been of the very best kind. My children didn't move house until they left to make their own. I wanted to make a family home, a place where we would stay, so they would have the opportunity to develop friendships that lasted, to have an education that wasn't broken at random points every few years, to have a home they could return to if they needed to when they left, and so we've been here since they were tiny and we are still here now. It is a tall, thin house with a cherry tree outside the front that I planted when it was little. Peggy writes by the window on the top floor and I work in the garden. I fulfilled my need to wander by gardening and hiking in the mountains for days on end, but now they are gone and I think I need another adventure—that is my Gipsy strain, more dilute in them than it is in me, and the time to pack up and move on will come soon, I can feel it in the air.

Becoming a father was never a plan. I thought I would be a very poor father, didn't know what a good father might be like. Sometimes in the mirror I would see my father's face and worry that I would be like him, as I believe he was like his. But they were soldiers, and I never was. They were born at the end of a war: authoritarians who believed in a power structure, a chain of command and knew their place in it. I don't believe in too many rules, and I think that might have helped me be a parent in some ways and been problematic in others. I didn't know how to discipline, or even if I should. I just made it all up as I went along. Often I got it wrong, they ended up crying, I ended up crying, we all ended up crying together. I only saw my father cry once. I cry at the drop of a hat. We laughed a lot, went camping, did art-things. We were dirt poor, but there was food of the poor sort. They are adults now, but still have friends they went to school with, who played here in this garden that has been in their time a playground, a campsite, a barbecue pit, a festival site, a nature walk, a place to store their bikes and a dumping ground for old car parts.

Now the garden is becoming again the woodland edge it used to be before this house, this street, this town was built. It didn't take long to design the structure of what goes where and why, but it will take at least two years for the plants to settle and behave as if they belong. Not long, in the scheme of things. Plants are often moved from one place to another, but it can disturb them greatly, slow or even stop their growth and some will not survive. People too can move, but I wanted to give my children something that I didn't have: a chance to set down some roots. None of these plants will be moved, and next year the foxgloves will be dense with older ones and youngsters, and the daffs and wild garlic will have spread in the spring and the ferns will unroll bigger and fuller. So in two or three years there will be new plants and new flowers, and others will find their own way here. Some of them, if the conditions are right, will thrive, some may just survive, while others will not grow at all in the battle for life that every garden is. I wonder if I will still be here. I'm old, but not too old to go wandering, and the nature of life is change.

An hour passes and the ground becomes drenched and puddles appear, and it thunders on the roof above me and I begin to drift into the storm and feel the wildness of what this place has become; the earth trembles, the leaves and branches thrash, and I feel a sense of joy to have made a place that is wild and uncivilised—it really works.

Settling dust, booze, mother, vagrancy

All things are dust, which settles in patterns and then, moved by the breeze, it settles into new patterns. They go north to live in a pub in a mining village. Nobody seems to be acting or playing any more, nobody wears glitter. Everything is a bit too real. He has six months left at school before he can leave, and so does everybody else in his class; the boys will go down the mines or to factories, and the girls to the mills or the bleach-works or will become hairdressers. The sons and daughters of shop and factory owners will go away to university. The children of doctors, solicitors and accountants go to a completely different school. There is no garden, no sea, no elephants, no trees, no fortune-tellers, no books. The surrounding hills are coal tips and slag heaps. There's an all-pervading feeling that his boyhood is nearly over.

He isn't happy, but knows he'll be okay, he will cope and has all the optimism of his fifteen years. His world has changed again and again, and time moves everything around; he's seen it now, its flow, the shock of change, of loss, of coping, learning something new, becoming something new again, and each time he gains a scar that makes him stronger. He tries to find out who he should be in this place, how to survive and find happiness here.

The boy takes the bus to school each morning and back home every night. He doesn't know how to make friends, his accent is odd, his clothes are strange, the other kids are wearing old school uniforms they have mostly grown out of, while he wears bits of his previous school uniform. They have all known each other for years, and for the first time he realises that there are tribes; he's never noticed this before, he is used to kids playing with other kids or playing happily on their own, but here your team is important: City or United, football or rugby. There are tribes, and he isn't in one. The girls and boys don't play together here. He is the 'pikey' and a loner, but he can write stories and draw; he draws the school and the houses, the pitheads and the miners, and in maths and sciences he fails and in art and biology and English he comes top of the class.

He works in the cellar of the pub after school, learns bar work, pulling pints for miners who play darts and dominoes, serving gin and whisky for the couples in the lounge bar, which has carpets and upholstered seats. He learns about beer and spirits and their effects, and how to make a G&T, a Pink Gin, a Pimm's Cup, a Gin & It. He pulls himself a pint of Guinness every day after school, tastes his first whisky, takes up smoking and draws pictures of the customers in the pub, and suddenly the weirdo is a bit of a celebrity and his pictures are framed and hung on the walls. Some of the miners offer a quid or two for their portrait and, delighted, he gives them away and draws more.

He enjoys his own company, doesn't say much; he likes to draw and, starving for words, he will read—as if they were pages from an encyclopaedia and filled with knowledge—anything he finds lying about, from a biscuit packet to a bus timetable, to a dusty book of cocktail recipes found in the storeroom. Now people have an explanation for his oddness, they can give him a label, which helps them understand that he is 'an artist'. 'No, I just like drawing,' he says, but begins to wonder about becoming an artist. The careers advisor counsels against it when he asks: no opportunities, no way to make a living; you'd have to go away to college and have no money for years, you'd need good grades, a family who support you, and then you would struggle to find a job. Much better to do it in your spare time and go into industry. And so he listens and does what seems sensible, and goes to work in the welding shop beside the canal and learns to manipulate steel and drive a crane.

HE DOES NOT SEE his mother for days on end because she is either asleep or in hospital. At first she cried; she didn't like the pub or the dark mining town, the coal dust on everything, the shops and the accents she didn't understand, and she took to her bed. Then she started to come down in the dark and the cold in her nightie, from the flat they lived in above the bar, and drink whisky until she could barely stand, and spend her days in bed, and slowly she died of asthma. He hears her in the night, struggling to pull some dusty pit-town air into her failing lungs, sees the blue lights of the quiet ambulance flashing on his bedroom wall and people speaking softly, firmly, kindly in the hall. The talk of nebulisers and oxygen bottles, and how expensive they are.

One morning, while he is at work outside in the frozen winter steelyard, welding a flange to a five-inch oil pipe and watching the ice on the rusty steel melt and race up the pipe to turn into steam, he lifts his mask and, through the drizzle and the darkness, against the whiteness of the open gate he recognises his father's father standing, breathing clouds like feathers that drift away, and watching. Why would he be here, so far away from home and visiting his work—a man he barely knows? And he knows he will not see his mother again. He is sixteen.

He explains to his boss that he has to go. Funny how a death is embarrassing. He makes his work-piece secure, disconnects the cables from his arc welder, drags it on its wobbly wheels across the mud and ice into the workshop, rolls up the cables and hangs them on a hook, with his welding mask and gloves. The men inside are wondering why he's packing up at eleven in the morning, saying nothing, watching the weirdo leave. He goes home to the flat above a pub that is no more empty than it had been before, already hollowed out with bitterness and loneliness.

'IT'S YOUR FAULT she is dead—your fault,' the Angry Dog drooled when he was drunk, 'you piece of shit.' The boy thought he was muttering to himself, but when he was sober the old Dog said, as cold as ice, 'You need to leave. I don't want you here, you are surplus to requirements. If it hadn't been for you, we wouldn't have argued, she would still be alive. Fuck off, I'm done with you, and don't come back.'

And so the boy was cast out of hell and learned, in the same statement, that his silent mother had been fighting his corner and he had never known.

THERE HAD BEEN a vagrant who visited the village, who stayed for a few weeks in the summer. He wore an overcoat and a trilby hat, an ancient dark wool suit with turn-ups, a V-necked jumper that may once have been green or brown, a shirt collar that at one time may have been white but was now charcoal, and a tie with a tiny knot poked above the V of his jumper. He slept in the bus shelter, and sometimes older men from the pub would bring him a beer. He often had blood on his face somewhere among the stubble. You could see that he tried to shave sometimes, to make himself presentable as best he could. People said that he was rich and had a house and a wife who beat him up, threw boiling water on him, stabbed him with a dinner fork; people said he was traumatised in a war, and some claimed to have known him when he left the army; people said all sorts of things. People like to tell stories. After a few weeks he wandered off and would not be seen again until the following August.

The boy packs his rucksack, leaves his key on the dressing table, sleeps on people's sofas for a while until the welcome wears out, sleeps on park benches and a half-sunken narrowboat, in an abandoned warehouse and tries to save enough for a deposit on a flat, but doesn't earn enough to pay the rent and so he walks away.

He is going to find his life or lose it. Doesn't care if he lives or dies. He walks to the countryside and wanders, falls in love again with the open air, the road he travels on, the life and death that happen next to him in fields and rivers. Brushing every day through plants and nature, wandering and looking—just being, and being nobody. Walking in silence and finding the deeper silence inside it. Wordless, he learns through doing that the body he calls his body is not his; it is nature expressing itself, exactly as it expresses the trees and the flowers and the flies, as an orchestra expresses itself through music. The mind that uses the words 'my body', 'my mind', is not his, either, it is nature expressing itself. There is no 'me', no 'mine' that is anything more than words. Body and mind and world are all expressions of the world, arising and passing like waves on the sea, like wind in the air—no more, no less—and he passes his days opening himself up to this. Every moment of his time is his own, none of it owned by anyone else. No two days are the same. He avoids people and sleeps under trees and next to lakes for nearly two years, finds some work now and then and wanders off again. Builds a beautiful way alone in the wild: he walks the hills and finds his deepest inner peace where life and death are of equal value. He asks what life is for, thinks about worth and worthlessness, finds no meaning in either. For his father, life meant fear and worry, anger at the world that failed to come up to his expectations. For his mother, it meant loneliness and misery. And so he chooses to give his life meaning, and the meaning he gives it is love and forgiveness.

ON HIS HAND beneath a tree a ladybird lands; her black fly-like wings are twice as long as her little body and, as he watches, they collapse into floppy pieces of lace, she lowers her wing-cases and, with her back legs, bundles her wings underneath, squeezing all the air out as she goes, like crushing a sleeping bag and stuffing it into its sack. 'So that's how she does it!' he thinks as he wanders along and the bug climbs his arm and, after hitching a ride for a while, she splits her red back in two and, at incredible speed, inflates her enormous wings and flies off.

A crow watches first from one black pearly eye and then from the other; he opens his massive shiny feathers and, with barely a single downward stroke, is up and gliding as if not by his own effort, but as if he were lifted by a string to where he can watch the boy. He lands on a fence post, where the lichen finds the cracks where it is always moist and brings the old, dead timber back to life. Noticing without judging creates tranquillity in the mind. The boy, just like the crow, spreads his wings and lifts. Eventually he finds a job on the railway, like his father and grand-father and uncle before him. Then, drawn into a bookshop that he passes on his way to work, he wanders the shelves, absorbing the vanilla of new books and the millions of ideas at his fingertips. Another great adventure begins: books, art college, Zen, politics, lovers, gardening, raising children, writing.

Paradise regained

READING IN the GARDEN

When you are at the beginning of life it looks like an adventure, but when you come to one end or another and look back, the story we tell seems inevitable. As if it were all preordained. To look back is to stop moving forward and split the past from the present. To look back is not to live, it is to tell a tale, the plot of which is pure opera: an odyssey with life and death and love and grief, and wonderful music and costumes and dance—we all have a tale like this. I have told mine and have been distracted from the simple reality of the moment for too long now. I have been at the front row for a while, the excited chap who comes to every performance with a cane and a bow tie and smiles too much and laughs at places that others think are inappropriate.

I remember telling a teacher, 'I don't care what happens to me' and she said, 'If that is the case, you will be very happy.' I don't remember much about my teachers, but what she said has stuck for nearly sixty years, and she was right. I love without desire and I am contented. Desire itself is just another word for unhappiness and I watch it come and go, without paying too much attention to it. I manage to find happiness, I conjure some up from whatever I have at hand: a rock; a passing wave or chattering people walking by; the smile of an old lady; the tiniest wren foraging under the pink flowers of the currant bush, where fat bees stop to sip; a fly sheltering from the rain under a leaf; or a book that makes me stop and think, then work to find my place again. Sometimes, in my darkest hours, I have to look a little harder—people can create a dark so fierce it hides the joy of simply being here—but I always manage to come back and find it. Joy is never somewhere else. I am sad for the life of the Angry Dog, for its fear and hatred. The way to be happy is to see that life is ridiculous and continually forgive. I am a deeply happy man.

Sometimes in the mirror, or reflected in a window, I see my father's face of course, for I am his son and his genes continue on—the same pattern of hair loss, the same domed skull—but he took a path of 'self' and 'me' and 'power', and his sickness eroded my own sense of self. A Buddhist would ask, 'What is good, what is bad? Each becomes and is, at one time, the other.' My lack of 'sense of self' gave me a clue to finding 'no-self'; it was the greatest gift I've ever had and I have polished my no-self for years. Sometimes I've forgotten about it, but it always comes back, because that is who I am—who we all are.

LIFE IS INFINITELY CREATIVE—gardening is the same as painting, as writing, as dancing. The garden I made is this book; this book I wrote is a garden. It is finished. This body is getting old. My hands sometimes shake a little now and I wonder for a moment if it's Parkinson's; my walking stick is well used and my hearing fades—I can't hear swifts any more with my ears, but I don't need to, I have them inside for ever.

It is everybody's job to blossom and flower, even unnoticed in shady corners. Just blossom. Each moment is movement; the river swells and eddies, breaks into waves and settles, urges and relaxes, but it is always the river, there is no other. All things move and nothing remains, but for a while, here in the shed in the rain and waiting for Peggy to let me in, I remember an island, a boy surviving tempests and shipwrecks, finding seeds and books, which, like Prospero, gave me the magic to conjure up infinite peace from the rocks and plants and insects and winds.

There is by the box of seed packets on my bench a candle, of course, surrounded with finds from the garden: snail shells, seashells, seed heads, twigs, a pine cone and a pebble that looks like a face. I like to build little altars wherever I go—altars to the joy of chaos. I light the candle with a match from the box that sits beside it and watch it fight for life, burn bright, then fail, then bright and tall again in the draught that comes around the door, which already doesn't fit quite as well as it did. I write in my notebook with a pencil stump. There is always a notebook and a pen or a pencil nearby, just in case. I write a little poem: writing poems helps me to find out what I think about things, to bring to the surface what is bubbling beneath. Sometimes they make a kind of sense.

All the moments arrive,
the past and present intertwine.
In this brief spell, the brief rose blooms and dies,
a brief life passes by, the brief trees grow and stand,
        then fall.

It is nearly dark, and the little flame sheds some light in this tiny space, as every life does. As the rain fades away, beyond the reflection of the flame in the window, the full moon shines on the vast dark sky and the raindrops on the window spark, and far away—so very far away—I see a boy in blue shorts, paddling an opal plastic tub across the dark and deadly sky. He is going away from me now, moving uncertainly but determined, on his own fabulous adventure to his future, to where we meet, here in this shed.

By the time I see the light go on in the kitchen that tells me Peggy is home, in the tall, thin house we have lived in for thirty-five years, I have written five pages. Some of what I have written is far too dark and sad. I'm feeling my way forward with it; I'm not at ease looking back—it isn't how I usually live and I'll probably throw a lot away and embellish what is left, add just a little bit of gloss. I'm not very good at making up stories in my head, like Peggy does, my mind doesn't work like that; but give me an outline and I'm good with glitter and show, and I can polish a clay tile until I can see my face in it. I think I'm writing a reflection in a mirror, a self-portrait in the best light—a selfie, light-filters applied. We are, after all, nothing more than the stories we tell ourselves, and they are always changing.

I blow out my candle and walk to the door and knock. When she sees me out in the dark, Peggy laughs and lets me in. 'You locked me out!' I say with faked distress, feeling that I more deserve pity than mockery.

She apologises, says, 'Oh God, I'm sorry. Have you been out there all this time?' Then she laughs some more.

She has brought gin, so I get out the cocktail glasses, olives, gin, vermouth, and make the most perfect Dirty

Martinis—I learned how to do this when I was a boy. I read to her what I have written. Tomorrow I'll write a little more at the kitchen table or at my desk. I've had enough of sheds and rotting hulks, I need comfort now and a different kind of adventure.

The mind is its own place and in itself,
can make a Heaven of Hell, a Hell of Heaven.

JOHN MILTON, *Paradise Lost*

This is the final book in my
'Gardener's Chronicle' trilogy:
How to Catch a Mole
Seed to Dust
Spring Rain

....

These are for you.
I wish you peace and happiness.

THE ENCYCLOPAEDIA

For the sake of full disclosure, although I searched long and hard to find a set of the original encyclopaedia that I discovered as a boy, I was unable to, nor was I able to recall the name or the edition—only the colour and format, the feel and heft and smell. So, for the sake of this book, I acquired from second-hand bookshops three different sets, which between them gave me the entries I was looking for. The rest of this book is substantively factual.

THE ILLUSTRATIONS

It felt fitting that I should illustrate this book myself, which (because I am old, and writing is hard and getting work published is difficult) may well be my final book. After many years of not drawing, I thought I would come back to it and close the circle. I have been sitting in my little garden and drawing the shed and the plants, freer now than my meticulous hard-won work when I was a boy, drawn hunched, with my lip between my teeth in concentration. Now I let it go of thoughts, of self, and a line arises, then another—it's fun, but I'd rather write, my hands are too shaky.

DEDICATION

I hope I have made a beautiful thing with these words. That's all I wanted: to add a little more to the wonder. As always, I struggle with the act of making beauty in an age of brutality, and even more with the ethics of focusing my attention on the wonder of life when there is so very much that needs changing. Can one overcome aggression with peace? I hope so. Helping me with the wonder were my beloved wife Peggy (Kate Hamer), my agent Robert Caskie and my editor Liz Foley, who all make appearances in the crowd scene outside the railway station at the beginning of the book (they weren't there in reality, but I added them for fun—we do like to tell stories!). And my publishers, Greystone Books, Harvill Secker and Vintage, with whom I am deeply proud to have the honour of working, because without a doubt they publish some of the greatest books in the world.

This book is also dedicated to my art teachers, Jean Gordon from Manchester Metropolitan, who taught me about colour, and Leslie Thornton from North Stafford-shire Polytechnic, who taught me about form—sadly, both now departed. I also had an English teacher at Fielden Park College of Further Education who was immensely encouraging about my writing when I returned to education at the age of twenty-four. She told me to keep on writing, keep on reading, keep on dancing. Unfortunately I cannot remember her name, only that she was twice my age, wore a tartan kilt and I fancied her like mad.

I also want to thank my friends Prof. Alan Lewis and Janet Sampson, whom I told about my partial encyclopaedia over too many bottles of rosé in the pub; they laughed at my much-embellished version and exaggerated misfortune and said I should write about it (one does not tell the darkest truths in the pub with friends).